The Degrees

W. David Crowl

ISBN-10: 0-86690-632-0
ISBN-13: 978-0-86690-632-6

Cover Design: Jack Cipolla

Published by:
American Federation of Astrologers, Inc.
6535 S. Rural Road
Tempe, AZ 85283

www.astrologers.com

Printed in the United States of America

Contents

Introduction

Degree symbolism is by no means an exact science. And yet this branch of astrology has haunted me for almost twenty-five years. The following descriptions of the degrees of the zodiac are often merely a confirmation of the work I have done and two excellent books on the subject: Donna Walter Henson's *Degrees of the Zodiac* and Esther V. Leinbach's *Degrees of the Zodiac*. But sometimes I agree and sometimes I disagree with them. The names of the fixed stars are included with the appropriate degree if I believe they contribute an influence to that degree. If a person's name is listed, his or her Sun is in that degree, unless otherwise specified. Some specifics:

- All beginning degrees are ego degrees. Not just Aries.
- All ending degrees have a difficulty. They are not characteristic of either the outgoing sign or the incoming sign, and sometimes they are a subtle blending of both.
- Middle degrees (15) are usually odd, and not really typical of the sign.
- All 13 degrees are unlucky. They have problems or make them. In addition, people who are born on the thirteenth day of any month are also not very fortunate in my experience, with the possible exception of May 13.

- All 3 degrees are powerful, and usually an area of genius. The 26 degrees are usually strong, too.
- All 20 degrees, except Virgo and Scorpio and sometimes Gemini, seem to come out as a kind of dead letter. (Or dead number, so to speak.) In other words, they are some of the weaker or less important degrees. This is in sharp contrast to many of the 19 degrees, which can be rather powerful or violent, especially Aries, Taurus, Virgo, Libra, Scorpio, and Capricorn.
- You can often observe a sort of "opposite poles" influence that is roughly the same in two degrees that are exactly opposed to one another—a sort of "boomerang effect" in the zodiac.

Strange and startling as it may sound, I do not find that the influence of the degrees has really changed in the last two thousand years. Marcus Aurelius' Sun in 5 Taurus is still a calm and harmonious degree for a philosopher, Michelangelo's Sun in 24 Pisces is still a painter's degree, and so on and so on around the zodiac. If I am living in error on this point, I should gladly welcome being corrected by another astrologer.

The reader should bear a few things in mind when using this book.

First, the degree that the Sun is in is always the most important degree and will say something about the native's identity in general. This is followed in importance by the Ascendant degree (provided you are sure of the correct birth time), which is of course another key to the personality. The Midheaven degree and the other two angles may also have an effect on the chart, but the Moon is third in significance and reveals something about the native's emotional nature.

Moreover, all ten of the planets will have an impact on the degree where they are situated according to the nature of that planet. If Mercury happens to fall upon a writing or teaching degree, this would be an excellent influence. Venus will soften a difficult degree or make it more friendly, and Mars will energize a weaker one or make it more aggressive, or perhaps sexual.

For example, if you find Venus located in 23 Capricorn, which can be a "tough customer" kind of degree, it will come out sweeter than if Mars is situated there. Jupiter will blow up or exaggerate or make lucky a particular degree, and Saturn will limit, hold down, or perhaps discipline one; Saturn sitting on a very active or fiery degree will thus not have the same influence as when Mars or Uranus is placed there.

In addition, Saturn, the Great Teacher, will often have some specific lesson to teach in the degree where it is located. Mercury or Uranus will make a mental degree even more mental, or possibly brilliant. Venus and Neptune will enhance the creativity of an artistic degree. And Pluto will of course increase the power or regenerative ability of any degree it comes in contact with.

Furthermore, the degrees where the North and South Nodes are located should be included as well. The North Node degree will often bring a benefit of some sort; the South Node degree may create a problem. Lastly, please keep in mind that these degree influences are not mathematically exact. By no means. You must often use a little leeway.

Another consideration is the aspects. The general rule here is that if the degree where a planet is located has a great many squares and oppositions from other planets, this will make it more difficult for a positive influence to emerge. And if the degree has a lot of trines and sextiles, the opposite is true.

Examples

The charts of media mogul Oprah Winfrey and U.S. President Barack Obama reveal a great deal of information about how degree symbolism works in action.

Oprah has the Sun in 8 Aquarius 59, which makes her a unique person; but since her Sun is only one second away from 9 Aquarius, she is also forceful but diplomatic. This degree is, in addition, good at dealing with people.

Her Ascendant is in 29 Sagittarius, which often denotes someone who wants to be the boss. This is a good degree for entertainers, who are especially concerned with their physical health and condition. Oprah, like Madonna, has her own personal trainer.

Next, her Midheaven is in 17 Libra, which is frequently involved with talking or debate and this is what she does in her media career. This degree strives to be the best.

Then we have the IC in 17 Aries, which often brings violence into the life. Oprah had a rough childhood and was sexually assaulted in her youth on more than one occasion.

(Notice that the Ascendant, Midheaven, and IC degrees are all good indications that we are dealing with an exact birth time. Indeed, by checking all four angles and sometimes the Moon, which changes its degree roughly every two hours, you can often use this degree book to confirm the accuracy of a horoscope.)

Oprah's Moon is in 4 Sagittarius, which shows real moral fiber and can even become quite righteously indignant at times. It also has the usual Sagittarian optimism and cheerfulness.

Her Mercury in 19 Aquarius is a sign of success in her chosen field. Her Venus in 8 Aquarius gives her a striking personality and makes her a thinker.

We find Oprah's Mars in 23 Scorpio, which brings luck with money, although they usually must earn it all themselves. Her Jupiter in 16 Gemini adds intelligence and artistic power. Her Saturn is in 9 Scorpio and this often eliminates one of the parents; Oprah was abandoned by both her parents at an early age and reared chiefly by her grandmother.

Perhaps her Uranus in 20 Cancer has less influence on her chart, but it is often a sign of intelligence. Her Neptune is in 26 Libra, which is an artistic degree, and Oprah has also been an actress in the past. Finally, her Pluto is in 24 Leo, a degree that indicates a great mother and love for protecting all things innocent and defenseless; sometimes it seems like she is the big mother of us all. This degree probably adds a little playfulness to her character as well.

Oprah's North Node is in 23 Capricorn and this can indicate a person who acts tough and direct on the outside but who is quite pleasant underneath. On the other hand her South Node is in 23 Cancer and this indicates someone who has worked her way up the ladder of success; no one can deny that she most certainly has done that. In conclusion, it should be quite clear that many details of Oprah's life are made evident through degree symbolism.

Barack Obama's Sun is in 12 Leo, which is a financially fortunate degree. He gets along well with people and there is something joyful and idealistic in the man that this degree appears to radiate.

Obama's Ascendant is in 18 Aquarius, which is one of the most brilliant Aquarius degrees. It often makes a writer and Obama is a successful author. His Midheaven is in 28 Scorpio, which seems to bring strange and fateful events into the life.

Next we find the Moon in 3 Gemini, which is another brilliant degree. Obama graduated *magna cum laude* from Harvard University, where he was also elected president of the prestigious *Harvard Law Review*.

His Mercury is in 2 Leo, a degree that indicates teaching ability (he was a teacher at the University of Chicago School of Law); this degree knows how to make difficult things easy to understand. His Venus in 1 Cancer makes him both a traveler and a family man. Mars in 22 Virgo is a degree that gets along well with the group, and of course every politician has need for this quality.

Jupiter is in 0 Aquarius, a degree that has many original ideas and perhaps vision and insight; it also has leadership potential. His Saturn is located in 25 Capricorn, which is a formal and conservative degree, very typical of Capricorn. And there is certainly a conservative note in his character. Who knows? Perhaps he even has a lesson to learn about not worrying about what the neighbors will think! His Uranus falls in 25 Leo, one of the "great lover" degrees, and this type of aura or influence is useful in political campaigning.

Obama's Neptune falls in 8 Scorpio in Obama's chart, and like 7 Scorpio, which precedes it, this can be a degree of strength and authority; moreover, this degree can be passionate and gives a good mind. His Pluto is in 6 Virgo, which is often in need of regeneration, but his Pluto is only one second away from 7 Virgo, a degree that adds honesty and moral grit to the character.

Lastly, Obama's North Node is in 27 Leo, which seems to bring a person the karma they deserve; perhaps in Obama's case, this comes out quite positively. On the other hand, his South Node is in 27 Aquarius, another sign of strength and intelligence.

And a last word of caution to the reader: I find degree symbolism to be a great astrological tool, but please do not overly emphasize it. Degree symbolism is not a substitute for a full horoscope analysis.

Finally, on a grander scale, this subject of degree symbolism will inevitably provoke serious questions in the mind of the astute reader. How large a role has chance played in my life? Upon my identity, my resources, my career, my destiny? Should I not be more tolerant and understanding of those who have been less fortunate than myself? Moreover, what can I realize and achieve in this life with the potential the stars have presented to me right from the moment of my birth?

Aries

0 Aries

Fire and energy! The life force. The first day of spring. The epitome of the ego and all the inherent selfishness that implies. Strong creative urge. The high energy of Aries and its ruling planet, Mars, are immediately apparent in the first four degrees of this sign.

Examples: composer Modest Mussorgsky, actor William Shatner, composer Stephen Sondheim.

1 Aries

More of the same as the first degree. The enthusiasm and impulsiveness continue. But with an artistic slant. *Joie de vivre*.

Examples: artist Van Dyck, impresario Florenz Ziegfeld, actor Chico Marx, director Akira Kurosawa, actor Karl Malden, actress Ali McGraw, singer Joan Baez (Ascendant).

2 Aries

The same energy and drive, yet now with a more scientific and sometimes even mathematical emphasis. These natives are often humorous. The comedian.

Examples: artist William Morris, astrologer-author Dane Rudhyar, psychologist Erich Fromm, actress Joan Crawford, comedian Dick Gregory (Moon), actor Paul Hogan (Jupiter).

3 Aries

The scientific thrust reaches a high point. Energy abounds. Impulsiveness, *élan vital* (vital force).

Examples: seer Nostradamus (Ascendant), philosopher Nietzsche (Uranus), mathematician Einstein (Mercury), historian A.J.P. Taylor, actress Sarah Bernhardt (Moon and Uranus), conducter Arturo Toscanini, actor Steve McQueen, bank robber Clyde Barrow, actress Simone Signoret, singer Elton John, singer Chaka Khan.

4 Aries

A good degree for singers. But something primitive, the animal instinct. Possibly cruel. The call of the wild. Music.

Examples: murderer Perry Smith (Uranus), singer Aretha Franklin, composer Bela Bartok, mathematician Einstein (Saturn), playwright Tennessee Williams, activist Gloria Steinem, reporter Howard Cosell, actress Marcia Cross, comedian-actor Paul De Leeuw.

5 Aries

Music. Many singers and poets. Torn between fear and cruelty. A great deal of frustration is at work in this degree. Knocking the wind out of his sails. A lost dream.

Examples: poet A. E. Housman, poet Robert Frost, Lucrezia Borgia (Moon), Henri Landru (Mercury), murderer Adolf Eichmann (Venus), reporter Bob Woodward, actor Alan Arkin, actor Michael York, singer Anita Bryant, author Erica Jong, composer Pierre Boulez.

6 Aries

The frustration continues. The ambitions are held back. Checkmate. A lesson in selflessness must be learned.

Examples: politician Albrecht von Wallenstein (Pluto), czar

Nicholas II (Jupiter), activist Che Guevarra (Uranus), politician Edmund Muskie, inventor Wilhelm Roentgen, actress Gloria Swanson, pianist Wilhelm Backhaus, actor James Caan, singer Diana Ross.

7 Aries

A good degree for dancers. They get along better with others. Tact and diplomacy is being learned. The diplomat.

Examples: U.S. President Abraham Lincoln (Venus), actor James Stewart (Saturn), poet Alfred de Vigny, dramatist Maxim Gorky, composer Ferde Grofe, singer Pearl Bailey, singer Sarah Vaughan, politician John Major, actress Elle Macpherson, model Tyra Banks (Moon), singer Lady Gaga.

8 Aries

The beggar's degree. Full of violence and feelings of vengeance. A lot of nastiness in this spot. Envy, impatience, or the desire to lord it over others. Fixed star Algenib.

Examples: farmer Billy Carter (brother of U.S. President Jimmy Carter), politician Eugene McCarthy, U.S. President John Tyler, actor Christopher Lambert, astrologer-author Alan Oken.

9 Aries

A strong desire to be Number One (first decanate of Aries). A good degree for painters. These people rush in.

Examples: murderer Hermann Goering (Mars), artist Francisco Goya, artist Vincent Van Gogh, artist Leonardo da Vinci (Mercury), psychologist B.F. Skinner, actor Warren Beatty, actor Brad Pitt (Jupiter), singer M.C. Hammer.

10 Aries

Good writer's degree. Sometimes a military leader. The commander-in-chief.

Examples: author Descartes, poet Paul-Marie Verlaine, author Nikolai Gogol, Emperor Maximilian I, politician Oliver Cromwell (Mars), revolutionary Leon Trotsky (Saturn), military leader Douglas MacArthur (Saturn), military leader George Marshall (Jupiter), statesman Otto von Bismark, actor Richard Chamberlain, politician Al Gore, composer Herb Alpert, actress Ali MacGraw, singer Celine Dion, activist Cesar Chavez.

11 Aries

Genius of one sort or another, but especially musical. A prodigy. Also science and mathematics. Unique individuals who are also very unpredictable.

Examples: composer Johan Sebastian Bach, composer Joseph Haydn, composer Erik Satie (Neptune), inventor Thomas Edison (Uranus), actor Robert Duvall (Uranus), scientist R.J. Oppenheimer (Venus), scientist Alfred Nobel (Pluto), author Simone de Beauvoir (Jupiter), author Hans Christian Andersen, actor Lon Chaney, actor Sir Alec Guinness, musician Leon Russell.

12 Aries

Rebellious types but also home-loving. They must follow their own path. A certain amount of selfishness is evident here. Very active. The Don Juan.

Examples: poet Edmond Rostand, industrialist Walter P. Chrysler, artist Max Ernst, politician Helmut Kohl, actress Debbie Reynolds, singer Marvin Gaye. Great lover and adventurer Giacomo Casanova.

13 Aries

High intelligence. Makes a good writer. Good intuition and an enormous ego. A primadonna. Danger from fire.

Examples: author Emile Zola, actor Eddie Murphy, actress Doris Day, singer Wayne Newton, astrologer Doris Chase Doane, military leader Douglas MacArthur (Ascendant) actor Marlon Brando (Moon), actor Leslie Howard, actor Heath Ledger.

14 Aries

Speedy types. Always on the move. A taxi driver. They lack warmth in human relationships and are always making their observations.

Examples: actor Steve McQueen (Venus), dancer Arthur Murray. author Washington Irving. Chris Costner Sizemore (woman with identity disorder), actor Tony Perkins, actor Marlon Brando.

15 Aries

Another strong musical degree. An orchestra conductor. Also art and acting. There is a strong conservative note here, and often spiritual power as well.

Examples: conductor Herbert van Karajan, singer Luciano Pavarotti (Moon), artist Raphael, author Algernon Swinburne, actress Bette Davis, actor Gregory Peck, actor Spencer Tracy, actor Gale Storm, philospher Moses Ben Maimon, philosopher Paramhansa Yogananda, philosopher Baba Ram Dass, author Descartes (Jupiter), astrologer Bessie Leo.

16 Aries

Music. There is a religious or spiritual interest. A saint. They are conservative but with an eccentric aspect to their nature.

Examples: singer Billie Holiday, composer Brahms (Ascendant), singer Merle Haggard, Saint Teresa of Avila, theosophist Annie Besant (Uranus), magician Aleister Crowley (Midheaven), author Booker T. Washington, aviator Anthony Fokker, commentator David Frost, director Francis Ford Coppola, actor Jackie Chan, actor Russell Crowe.

17 Aries

Poetic and passionate. Romeo and Juliet. Good imagination. Many journalists. A potential for violence in the chart of the attacker or the victim. Homicidal tendency. A love of luxury and extravagance.

Examples: reporter Lowell Thomas, actress Ilka Chase, King Richard III (Mars), murderer John Wilkes Booth (Pluto), military leader George Custer (Pluto), bank robber Jesse James (Uranus), Queen Mary I (Neptune), murderer Henri Landru (Neptune), actress Natalie Woods (Saturn), murderer Perry Smith (Moon), actor Rex Harrison (Moon), singer Whitney Houston (Moon), actor James Garner, philosopher Charles Fourier, singer Franco Corelli, singer Jacques Brel, fashion designer Vivienne Westwood, politician Gerhard Schroeder.

18 Aries

A poet's degree. The lyricist. Also a potential for being either sexually passionate or physically violent.

Examples: poet William Wordsworth, King Leopold II, gangster Bugsy Siegel (Mars), commentator Walter Winchell, composer Antal Dorati, singer Walter Berry, First Lady Betty Ford, actress Patricia Arquette.

19 Aries

A dark degree in one way or another. Erotic or over-sexed. The decadent. There is an element of tragedy here that may be due to a lower standard of morality, which seems strange and paradoxical because this degree is the exaltation point of the Sun. Mental fertility.

Examples: Philip IV of Spain, poet Baudelaire, publisher Hugh Hefner, singer John Lennon, singer Bette Midler (Ascendant), author Francis Bacon (Jupiter), publisher Joseph Pulitzer, actor Jean-Paul Belmondo.

20 Aries

A weak degree in general. Much activity with little accomplished. Here, there, and everywhere. Need to learn to look before they leap. Sometimes lucky.

Examples: Actor William Booth, actor Omar Sharif, author Paul Theroux, astrologer-author Linda Goodman, actor Steven Seagal.

21 Aries

Also not a particularly strong or interesting degree. The ne'er-do-well. Perhaps a traveler.

Examples: Wallis Simpson, Duchess of Windsor (Mars), comedian David Letterman.

22 Aries

This is one of the most brilliant degrees of Aries. A big ego and artistic talent. However, here we also find people who cannot make up their minds, possibly a polar influence from Libra in the same degree. The inventor. Extremely active.

Examples: U.S. President Thomas Jefferson, scholar Thomas Malthus (Uranus), author Fyodor Dostoyevsky (Jupiter), philosopher Friedrich Nietzsche (Pluto), artist Robert Delaunay, playwright Samuel Beckett, murderer Henri Landru, singer Monserrat Caballe, astrologer-author Howard Sasportas.

23 Aries

This, too, is one of the most brilliant degrees of Aries. Profound, contemplative, and philosophical. Also an innovator. There is, moreover, a strong sexual need, and they experience problems with the opposite sex. Sex appeal.

Examples: politician Henry Clay, chess champion Garry Kasparov, attorney Clarence Darrow (Jupiter), author Marcel Proust (Neptune and Ascendant), theologian Paul Tillich

(Moon), author Liz Renay, actress Julie Christie, politician Francois Duvalier, banker Roberto Calvi.

24 Aries

Here the sexual need is increased, and artistic endeavors should be encouraged. This degree also illustrates Freud's theory of the sublimation of erotic energy. The charmer.

Examples: actor Rod Steiger, actress Claudia Cardinale, actress Samantha Fox, actress Heather Lochlear (Moon), actress Charlize Theron (Jupiter), artist Michelangelo (Venus), sociologist Emile Durkheim, historian Arnold Toynbee.

25 Aries

The ambition and arrogance of Aries rises to a peak in this degree. These people wish to make an impression upon the world. The social climber. There is a desire to travel.

Examples: U.S. President Andrew Jackson (Ascendant), author Henry James, artist Vincent Van Gogh (Mercury), dictator Adolf Hitler (Mercury), actor Peter Ustinov, First Lady Jacqueline Kennedy (Moon), actress Elizabeth Montgomery.

26 Aries

Beginning in this degree, the sign Aries becomes more militant and aggressive. This degree and the next would be good for a military leader. These people also wish to rise in the ranks. The careerist.

Examples: author George Sand (Moon), bank robber Jesse James (Pluto), German President Paul von Hindenburg (Pluto), philosopher Thomas Hobbes, Pope Benedict XVI, artist Ford Madox Brown, author Anatole France, aviator Wilbur Wright, composer Henry Mancini, composer James Last, commentator Harry Reasoner, athlete Kareem Abdul-Jabbar, actress Olivia Hussey, fashion designer Victoria Beckham.

27 Aries

This degree is also aggressive. They are fighters. They show no weakness. The fearless warrior.

Examples: financier J.P. Morgan, actor Charlie Chaplin, Russian Premier Nikita Khrushchev, actor William Holden, U.S. President Andrew Jackson (Uranus), politician Maximilien de Robespierre (Moon), murderer Henri Landru (Moon), gangster Al Capone (Moon), author Karen Blixen, actor James Woods.

28 Aries

A lighter side of Aries comes in, perhaps already the influence of Taurus. An idyll. A more idealistic bent. An artistic side. Musical.

Examples: Composer Giuseppe Verdi (Moon), attorney Clarence Darrow, conductor Leopold Stokowski, actor Dudley Moore, actor Charlie Tuna, actress Hayley Mills, venture capitalist Philippe Junot.

29 Aries

An almost domestic element. More idealism. A certain peaceful strength. The best possible combination of Aries and Taurus. Smooth as silk.

Examples: Emperor Napoleon III (Sun and Mars), actress Jayne Mansfield, actress Ashley Judd, actress Kate Hudson.

Taurus

0 Taurus

Strong personality and ego. Prophet of a new order. Battle of the sexes. There is a selfish element here which does not make for smooth one-to-one relationships.

Examples: Queen Elizabeth II, dictator Adolf Hitler, artist Odilon Redon, artist Joan Miro, Prince Charles (Moon), actress Brigitte Bardot (Uranus), actor Ryan O'Neal, author Alistair MacLean, psychologist Rollo May, actress Jessica Lange, Carmen Electra.

1 Taurus

The selfishness of 0 Taurus continues. People who try to protect themselves at all costs, which often results in loneliness. The law of self-preservation. However, they can also be high-minded.

Examples: Queen Catherine de Medicis, author Madame de Stael, author Charlotte Bronte, scientist Robert Oppenheimer, author Vladimir Nabokov, singer Peter Frampton.

2 Taurus

An intellectual influence begins in this degree. A deep thinker. Also an artistic side is evident.

Examples: Joseph Turner, conductor Yehudi Menuhi, actor Lee Majors, actor Anthony Quinn, singer Glen Campbell, singer

Sandra Dee, actor Jack Nicholson, philosopher Immanuel Kant, revolutionary Vladimir Lenin.

3 Taurus

This is the strongest area of genius in Taurus. The Renaissance man. Actors, singers, and dramatic writers. A big imagination, and one of the luckiest degrees of the zodiac. Also with money.

Examples: artist Leonardo da Vinci, philosopher Bertrand Russell (Mercury), actress Shirley Temple, actress Shirley MacLaine, singer Roy Orbison, singer Barbara Streisand, politician Stephen A. Douglas, composer Sergei Prokofiev, artist Willem de Koning, activist Michael Moore.

4 Taurus

A macho influence. Difficult to get along with. Perhaps repressed emotionally. They are too hard on others. Nevertheless, there may be a scientific influence.

Examples: singer Tom Jones (Jupiter), actor Al Pacino (Saturn), athlete Johan Cruyff, inventor Guglielmo Marconi, military leader Henri Petain, commentator Edward R. Murrow, artist Karel Appel, murderer Josef Mengele (Saturn).

5 Taurus

One of the most beautiful degrees in Taurus. Serenity, patience, composure, and diplomacy, all the best of the Taurean qualities. The philosopher. Often a singer because this degree rules the vocal chords. There is a steady, quiet approach, a desire for harmony, and an interest in the occult. They hurt no one. A very musical area begins here and continues for the next five degrees, especially for singers. "What is the present estate of my understanding? For herein lieth all indeed."—Marcus Aurelius.

Examples: Emperor Marcus Aurelius, philosopher Rene Descartes (Moon and Venus), author A.C. Doyle (Mercury), author Aldous Huxley (Moon), author Walter de la Mar, actor Al

Pacino, singer Shirley Bassey (Uranus), singer Joan Baez (Jupiter), poet Walt Whitman (Venus), actress Carol Burnett, actress Renee Zellweger.

6 Taurus

Makes a powerful leader. But also makes an enemy or two. The adversary. Willpower and stubbornness are getting started here. There is also a mental influence. Singers.

Examples: military leader U.S. Grant, U.S. President Franklin Delano Roosevelt (Saturn), dictator Fidel Castro (Mars), activist Coretta Scott King, artist Vincent Van Gogh (Uranus), military leader Ernst Roehm (Moon), scientist Charles F. Richter, philosopher Ludwig Wittgenstein, politician Rudolf Hess, singer Anne Murray (Mars), singer Bobby Darin (Uranus), singer Ricky Nelson (Saturn), composer Francis Lai.

7 Taurus

The stubbornness is deeply rooted here and in the following degree. It is impossible to change their minds. Dead weight or an immovable object. The sluggard. A fatalistic influence. Music. Fixed star Hamal.

Examples: Duchess Lucrezia Borgia, U.S. President James Monroe, inventor Samuel Morse, philosopher Herbert Spencer, military leader Wellington (Uranus), dicatator Joseph Stalin (Neptune), Queen Catherine the Great (Mars), singer Joan Sutherland (Ascendant), actress Ann-Margret, singer Prince (Venus), dictator Saddam Hussein.

8 Taurus

The same heavy influence as 7 Taurus. They must learn to control their tempers, and they are contrary, defensive, and stubborn. A bull in a china shop. It is said that people who have this degree are very fond of food. Singers. Some very attractive women.

Examples: military leader Georges Boulanger, publisher William R. Hearst, Emperor Hirohito (Sun and Venus), singer Placido Domingo, singer Frank Zappa, singer Neil Diamond (Saturn), singer Barbara Streisand (Mercury), conductor Duke Ellington, actress Michelle Pfeiffer, actress Uma Thurman, actress Jessica Alba, musician Toots Thielmans, actor Jerry Seinfeld, Zubin Mehta.

9 Taurus

Not an easy degree. The slave to the family. Stubbornness or defensiveness. They often go off half-cocked. Many singers.

Examples: Politician Joachim von Ribbentrop, Queen Juliana (Sun and Venus), singer Willie Nelson, singer Buddy Holly (Uranus), singer Jim Morrison (Moon), singer Tom Jones (Saturn)

10 Taurus

A very sensual degree. But also ability for science or mathematics. The epicurean. They very much like to enjoy themselves and are consequently in need of discipline. There is a certain lack of human sympathy.

Examples: Pediatrician Benjamin Spock, composer Franz Lehar, actor Glenn Ford, singer Rita Coolidge, singer Judy Collins, actress Joanna Lumley, fashion designer Donatella Versace.

11 Taurus

This degree lacks integrity. They are determined to get to the top by hook or by crook. The opportunist. Nevertheless there is a great deal of strength. Excessive ambition may bring about their downfall.

Examples: Queen Catherine the Great, Archduchess Maria Therese (Venus), Duke of Wellington, philosopher Teilhard de Chardin, Emperor Napoleon (Uranus), politician Cecil Rhodes (Uranus), comedian Jack Paar, athlete David Beckham.

12 Taurus

This degree is much more pleasant. Sweetness and light. "Pollyanna." Again the best of Taurus shines through here. However they certainly have their sensuous side.

Examples: singer Bing Crosby, William of Orange, the "red baron" Manfred von Richthofen, actress Mary Astor, columnist Hedda Hopper, politician Moshe Dayan, singer Frankie Valli, athlete The Rock.

13 Taurus

Taurean business sense begins to enter the picture with this degree. Salesmanship. But also acting and the stage. The bard. However there is also a certain paranoia: they are constantly feeling insulted whether this is the truth of the matter or not. Makes an intellectual.

Examples: author William Shakespeare (the traditional birthday choice of April 23), politician Oliver Cromwell, actress Audrey Hepburn, athlete Sugar Ray Robinson, philosopher Karl Marx, biologist Thomas Huxley, poet W.B. Yeats (Venus and Pluto).

14 Taurus

Good business sense. Money is important to them. A charming personality and good will toward others. The nice man or woman.

Examples: actor Michael Palin, actress Meryl Streep (Moon), actor Orson Welles, actor Tyrone Power, actor Stewart Granger, terrorist Brendt Andreas Baader.

15 Taurus

Another strong degree of Taurus. High intelligence. Also a business area. They are sympathetic. A good listener.

Examples: politician Maximilien Robespierre, First Lady Eva Peron, actor Rudolph Valentino, athlete Willie Mays, politician Tony Blair, actor George Clooney.

16 Taurus

A strong musical degree. The composer. They are headstrong but very talented. A powerful intellect can be found here, too.

Examples: composer Brahms, composer Tchaikovsky (Sun and Mars), philosopher David Hume, psychiatrist Sigmund Freud, explorer Robert E. Peary, actress Anne Baxter, actor Gary Cooper, actor Fernandel, author Rabindranath Tagore, director Roberto Rossellini, artist Ernst Kirchner, murderer Susan Atkins.

17 Taurus

A violent side of Taurus starts here. A ruffian. But some are artists or poets.

Examples: poet Robert Browning, poet Paul Verlaine (Mars), poet Ted Hughes (Moon), singer Ricky Nelson.

18 Taurus

Often called "the degree of unfoldment," some of these people rise from rags to riches. Nevertheless there can be a very violent and aggressive nature harbored here.

Examples: Sir James Barrie, industrialist Henry Kaiser, philosopher Ortega y Gasset, conductor Carlo Maria Giulini, athlete Pancho Gonzales, singer Ritchie Valens (Saturn), U.S. President Harry Truman, U.S. President John Kennedy (Mars), actress Glenda Jackson, singer Donovan, singer Billy Joel, actress Candice Bergen, activist John Brown.

19 Taurus

The self-made man or woman. A powerful but also violent degree of Taurus. The assassin. They make good dancers, and have other artistic abilities. Normally, they attain happiness in their lives.

Examples: biologist Thomas Huxley (Mars), politician Leland Stanford (Saturn), military leader U. S. Grant (Ascendant), U.S.

President James Garfield (Moon), astrologer Karl Ernst von Krafft, murderer John Wilkes Booth, murderer Mark David Chapman, director David O. Selznick, singer Bono, singer Sid Vicious, astrologer William Lilly, comedian Mort Sahl, astrologer Neil Michelsen.

20 Taurus

Boring and weak. Somehow jealous or envious of others, which is more of a Scorpio quality, belonging to the opposite sign. A jaundiced eye. Dancers.

Examples: philosopher Machiavelli, dancer Fred Astaire, dancer Martha Graham, composer Irving Berlin, artist Salvador Dali.

21 Taurus

Much stronger. Various talents. Suspicious and overly concerned with his security. On the safe side.

Examples: nurse Florence Nightingale, author Dante Gabriel Rossetti, composer Gabriel Faure, athlete Joe Louis, athlete Yogi Berra, actress Katharine Hepburn, singer Steve Winwood.

22 Taurus

The Sabian symbol "white dove over troubled waters" comes out here. All that is positive in Taurus returns. Home-loving. Plus a certain degree of ambition. They feel they have a mission to accomplish. Both creative and philosophical.

Examples: Queen Maria Therese, revolutionary Leon Trotsky (Mars), military leader Douglas MacArthur (Mars), Chairman Mao (Jupiter), psychic Edgar Cayce (Pluto), singer Joan Baez (Uranus), politician Yasser Arafat (Moon), cult leader Jim Jones, artist Edward Lear, artist Georges Braque, singer Ritchie Valens, singer Stevie Wonder, perhaps even philosopher Socrates.

23 Taurus

A strong, confident degree. Spiritual. Maybe lucky with money. The master of his or her fate.

Examples: conductor Otto Klemperer (Sun, Moon, Neptune), actor Joseph Cotton, politician Richard J. Daley, singer Bobby Darin, activist Che Guevara, director George Lucas.

24 Taurus

A steady Taurean degree. Pleasant and charming to everyone. After one's own heart.

Example: singer Trini Lopez.

25 Taurus

An intelligent and determined individual. Mathematics. But these people have a superiority complex and must learn that this may not be justified. Living in an ivory tower. Can bring violence.

Examples: musician Liberace, actor Henry Fonda, actor Jean Gabin, singer Birgit Nilsson, singer Anita Bryant (Mars), politician Ariel Sharon (Moon), actress Debra Winger, actress Tori Spelling, singer Ritchie Valens (Uranus), singer John Lennon (Uranus), politician Metternich.

26 Taurus

A sweet degree. However, Algol, the most violent star in the heavens, is located here, so they should be generally cautious and alert and avoid potentially dangerous situations.

Examples: composer Erik Satie, ballerina Margot Fonteyn, artist Vincent Van Gogh (Moon), Empress Alexandra (Mercury), revolutionary Leon Trotsky (Pluto), actor Will Rogers (Pluto), singer Ritchie Valens (Jupiter), activist Huey Newton (Uranus), politician Ruhollah Khomeini, actor Dennis Hopper.

27 Taurus

A spiritual or occult influence. Religion. A prelate.

Examples: Pope John Paul II, theologian Paul Tillich (Neptune), theologian James Pike (Saturn), psychic Elsie Wheeler's ascendant, politician Ho Chi Minh, director Frank Capra.

28 Taurus

A scientific or mathematical degree. Hard drinkers. Nevertheless they reveal powerful and magnetic personalities and are to be reckoned with. A proud and stoical element as well. Can bring suffering into the life. The stoic. Sometimes blindness.

Examples: Czar Nicolas II, dictator Tito, philosopher Bertrand Russell, activist Malcolm X, actor James Stewart, singer Joe Cocker, author John Milton (Moon).

29 Taurus

These people are aloof. Hoity-toity. The snob. Often makes a good writer. A stubborn streak makes them difficult to change. Also an actor's degree. Sometimes eye problems.

Examples: Revolutionary Toussaint L'Ouverture, politician Oliver Cromwell (Venus), composer Richard Wagner (Venus), actress Bette Davis (Mars), singer Cher, author Balzac, author John Stuart Mill, bullfighter El Cordobes, actor Lawrence Olivier, biochemist Ida Rolf.

Gemini

0 Gemini

A quick intelligence. Busy with themselves and anxious for the nice things of life, probably an influence from the Taurean cusp. Each of the twelve signs begins with a big ego. Interested in and good with small details. The perfectionist.

Examples: author Arthur Conan Doyle, author Vance Packard, astrologer Lois Rodden, poet Dante Alighieri, composer Richard Wagner, artist Henri Rousseau, singer Charles Aznavour, model Naomi Campbell, politician Harvey Milk, cartoonist Herge.

1 Gemini

Friendship is important. They are sticklers for details. Clever, but there is always something eccentric about their cleverness. A close friend.

Examples: physician Franz Mesmer, actor Douglas Fairbanks, fashion designer Aldo Gucci, actress Rosemary Clooney, Carolus Linnaeus.

2 Gemini

Solid as the Rock of Gibraltar. Steadiness. There seems to be still an influence from Taurus in this degree. You can count on them. Simple natural kindness of a child and yet they wish to make their mark on the world.

Examples: Queen Victoria, artist Mary Cassatt, military leader J.C. Smuts, astrologer Alexander Ruperti.

3 Gemini

True genius area of Gemini. Great depth, insight, and strength. The man of intellect. They may have a vast influence over others. Also a strong music degree. They have a great feeling for beauty.

Examples: poet Ralph Waldo Emerson, novelist Edward Bulwer-Lytton, philosopher Karl Marx (Mercury), poet Yeats (Mercury), author Jane Austen (Uranus), author Anton Chekov (Uranus), author Arthur Conan Doyle (Uranus), composer Monteverdi, singer Bob Dylan, musician Miles Davis, singer Beverly Sills, actress Priscilla Presley.

4 Gemini

The eagle eye. A degree of sharp observation and keen awareness. Nothing passes them by. Yet also a strong desire for status and recognition. Usually successful in their endeavors.

Examples: author Edmond de Goncourt, author George Washington Carver, boxer Gene Tunney, actor John Wayne, actor Vincent Price, actor James Arness, politician Henry Kissinger, astronaut Sally Ride.

5 Gemini

The speed freak. This is a very nervous, excitable degree. You will often find them running around like chickens with their heads cut off. And they enjoy this excitement very much. There is some writing ability.

Examples: actress Norma Talmadge, dancer Isadora Duncan, biologist Rachel Carson, actor Christopher Lee, astrologer Vivian Robson, athlete Sam Snead, singer Peggy Lee, singer Stevie Nicks, singer John Denver (Mars and Uranus).

6 Gemini

This is a powerful writing area. Also grammar. The mind ticks like a computer. Some are researchers. The writer.

Examples: author Ian Fleming, author William Shakespeare (Neptune), musician Cole Porter (Neptune), author J. R. R. Tolkien (Neptune), author Agatha Christie (Neptune), author Henry MIller (Neptune), author Honore de Balzac (Jupiter), author John Milton (Uranus), author James Barrie (Uranus), author Henry David Thoreau (Venus), author Vance Packard (Mercury), politician William Pitt the Younger, financier Jay Gould, singer Kylie Minogue.

7 Gemini

Can be a writing area, but chiefly these people are only concerned with themselves. The observer. They watch others and remain uninvolved. Also a fondness for money.

Examples: athlete Jim Thorpe, comedian Bob Hope, U.S. President John F. Kennedy, singer Gladys Knight, politician Rudy Giuliani, athlete Al Unser.

8 Gemini

This degree and the following one is a pain area in Gemini. Deafness. Also quite aggressive. They should probably make physical activity a priority in order to drain off excess energy. Commercial talent. The aggressor.

Examples: mining magnate Cecil Rhodes (Mars), industrialist Henry Kaiser (Venus), engineer John DeLorean (Moon), artist Albrecht Durer, poet Walt Whitman, Prince Rainier, transsexual Christine Jorgensen, actor Clint Walker, actor Michael J. Pollard, would-be murderer John Hinckley.

9 Gemini

Pain. Good at business. The entrepreneur. These people are very self-protective and take good care of their own interests. Sometimes a good imagination. Fixed star Aldebaran.

Examples: athlete Joe Namath, singer Peter Yarrow, actor-director Clint Eastwood, director R.W. Fassbinder. (Aldebaran).

10 Gemini

The world citizen. People with this degree care for the downtrodden, wants to save humanity. There is a clear idealism shining through here. Seems also to at times indicate an actor/actress.

Examples: religious leader Brigham Young, composer Mikhail Glinka, actress Marilyn Monroe, model Brooke Shields, actor Andy Griffith, singer Pat Boone, actor Colin Farrell.

11 Gemini

These people are talkative and high-strung, which are typical Gemini qualities. And they often miss out on life's rewards. Tough luck. There is also a sarcastic note. They sometimes seem oblivious or to lack understanding. Architects.

Examples: actress Sally Kellerman, occultist Count Alessandro di Cagliostro, author Thomas Hardy, athlete Johnny Weismuller, poet Allen Ginsberg, murderer David Berkowitz, serial killer Peter Sutcliffe.

12 Gemini

Often sarcastic. Also restless and always on the move. They have big plans and high expectations. Some are writers. The satirist.

Examples: Marquis de Sade, entertainer Josephine Baker, actor Tony Curtis, actor Stacy Keach.

13 Gemini

This degree is even more restless than the previous one. They are always tearing around. The misfit. Always travelling. They bear grudges and must learn patience in their relationships.

Examples: King George III, actress Rosalind Russell, actor Dennis Weaver, actor Noah Wyle, actress Angelina Jolie.

14 Gemini

The big liar degree. Many of these people have a hard time telling the truth about anything. Still, they have a fast mentality and with all this fantasy they may end up as writers. Frequently jump from one job to another.

Examples: murderer Josef Goebbels (Pluto), media mogul Martha Stewart (Jupiter), poet Frederico Garcia Lorca, actor Peter Lorre, comedian Bob Hope (Mercury), author John Maynard Keynes, actor Mark Wahlberg.

15 Gemini

A great teacher's degree. Learning in all forms, one of the most noble of Gemini's qualities. Could make a poet. There is a great deal of curiosity here. The teacher.

Examples: author Alexander Pushkin, author Thomas Mann, author Jean-Jacques Rousseau (Mercury), revolutionary Pancho Villa.

16 Gemini

Intelligent and artistic. Singers. Also more teachers. Perhaps they are over-sensitive. Wears the heart on his or her sleeve. Moreover, beginning in this degree the lungs become weaker—these people, especially, should not smoke!

Examples: artist Paul Gaugin, comedian Joan Rivers, singer Dean Martin, singer Tom Jones, singer Prince, athlete Bjorn Borg, astrologer Grant Lewi.

17 Gemini

There is enthusiasm, passion, and artistic imagination with this degree. Don't smoke! The romantic artist.

Examples: King Charles II, composer Robert Schumann, singer Nancy Sinatra, architect Frank Lloyd Wright, First Lady Barbara Bush, singer Amy Winehouse (Ascendant).

18 Gemini

This is probably the most brilliant degree of all Gemini. A swift intelligence and a myriad of interests. A high IQ. There is often creative power. The mind quickly penetrates to the essence of the matter. The possibility of asthma or pneumonia—thus, don't smoke!

Examples: Czar Peter the Great, artist Gustave Coubert, musician Cole Porter, singer Judy Garland, actor Robert Cummings, actor Michael J. Fox, actor Johnny Depp, Ben Jonson (Venus), author George Sand (Mercury), economist John Maynard Keynes (Mercury), author Rudhyar Kipling (Moon), U.S. Secretary of Defense Robert S. McNamera, astronomer Copernicus (Saturn), publisher William Randolph Hearst (Uranus).

19 Gemini

Far less brilliant than the previous degree. Often a good worker bee. Again, don't smoke. A shrew.

Example: singer Rise Stevens.

20 Gemini

This degree is full of curiosity, but they had better watch out! It sometimes makes a true leader. But they should be very careful with experimenting with drugs. Curiosity killed the cat.

Examples: Politician Cosimo de Medici, military leader George Patton (Ascendant), artist John Constable, composer Richard Strauss, author Anne Frank, author William Styron, actor Gene Wilder.

21 Gemini

One of the most scattered and restless degrees in Gemini. They must learn to discipline themselves. Nevertheless, this degree gives mental power, sometimes musical or mathematical ability, and has an unhappy influence on marriage. A marriage on the rocks.

Examples: Prince Aly Khan, Sir Anthony Eden, U.S. President George H. W. Bush.

22 Gemini

These people spread a lot of good will and harmony. Talent for math. A pleasant disposition.

Examples: First Lady Martha Washington, poet W. B. Yeats, actor Burl Ives, actress Xaviera Hollander, financier Donald Trump, singer Boy George, actress Mary-Kate Olsen, actress Ashley Olsen.

23 Gemini

Castles in the air. These people seem to have wild expectations that often don't work out. Still, they tend to remain optimistic. Mathematical ability.

Examples: astronomer J. E. Bode (Ascendant), psychiatrist Alois Alzheimer, astrologer John Addey, author Pierre Salinger.

24 Gemini

This is supposed to be a friendly degree. They can be overly ambitious. Career success. The confident smile.

Examples: astrologer Regiomontanus, composer Edvard Grieg, poet Joyce Carol Oates.

25 Gemini

Good dancers. An interest in astrology begins here. Some mental ability. An esoteric.

Examples: theosophist Alice Bailey, composer Charles Gounod, fashion designer Nicola Trussardi, Jean Pierre Peugeot, singer Barry Manilow.

26 Gemini

The last truly brilliant degree in Gemini. It inclines to artistic genius, especially music. The inspired one. They tend to have a refined nature, but they are also conformists.

Examples: composer Igor Stravinsky, singer Paul McCartney, singer Alison Moyet, singer Julio Iglesias (Saturn), author Thomas Paine (Neptune), author Charles Dickens (Jupiter), author Sylvia Porter, author Sartre (Mercury), actor Richard Boone, director Alfred Hitchcock (Neptune), author Stephen King (Uranus), author Salmon Rushdie, athlete Venus Williams, artist M. S. Escher.

27 Gemini

A contradictory influence: they are great travelers but also love their homes and countries. This is the struggle between Gemini and Cancer, which is just coming in. The last five degrees of Gemini is an astrology area; the Aquarian influence in the third decanate of Gemini probably explains this interest in the stars. Proud of their family. Gathers souvenirs and mementoes. The antique collector.

Examples: mathematician Pascal, composer Jacques Offenbach, politician Edouard Daladier, psychiatrist Immanuel Velikovsky, astrologer Dane Rudhyar (Jupiter), actor Errol Flynn, musician Guy Lombardo, actress Gena Rowlands.

28 Gemini

A love of travel or simply a love of nature. They can never sit still, have many good ideas, and often work long through the night. The workaholic.

Examples: sculptor Auguste Rodin (Moon), artist Vincernt Van Gogh (Jupiter), actor James Stewart (Mars), actor Peter O'Toole (Mars), actor Sean Connery (Mars), singer Barbara Streisand (Mars), military leader Douglas Haig, singer Chet Atkins, singer Anne Murray, singer Paula Abdul.

29 Gemini

Actors and entertainers. Also many writers. Often makes for a strong woman. There is a knowledge of human nature here, but they sometimes have a cruel side. The sadist.

Examples: actress Nicole Kidman, actress Juliette Lewis, author Ben Jonson, author Sartre, author Francoise Sagan (Sun and Mercury), actress Jane Russell, Duchess Wallis Simpson, politician Benazir Bhutto, bank robber John Dillinger, murderer Heinrich Himmler (Neptune), murderer Susan Atkins (Venus), model Naomi Campbell (Venus), terrorist leader Osama bin Laden (Moon), artist Rockwell Kent.

Cancer

0 Cancer

Large, healthy egos. Selfish. Something artistic, sensitive, or refined. Writers. They will try to get away with murder if you allow them to. A wolf in sheep's clothing.

Examples: author Anne Morrow Lindbergh, singer Judy Holliday, actress Meryl Streep (Sun and Uranus), author Rudhyar Kipling (Ascendant), author James Thackeray (Moon), author H. Rider Haggard, author Mary McCarthy, Prince William.

1 Cancer

Torn between travel and the home, between Gemini and Cancer. In general, friendly. Rather lucky. Stoke the home fires first—or else "hit the road, Jack" (a song by Ray Charles).

Examples: Empress Josephine (Sun and Mars), author Erick Maria Remarque, singer Kris Kristofferson, athlete Wilma Rudolph, director Paul Verhoeven.

2 Cancer

A spoiled child. Always has his or her reasons for taking action. Ambitious and with the memory of a professor or a scientist. A good writing degree.

Examples: Musician George Michael, author Mary Shelley (Ascendant), author George Orwell (Sun and Moon), author Andre

Gide (Moon), author Dylan Thomas (Saturn and Pluto), Duke of Windsor, Lord Kitchener, athlete Jack Dempsey.

3 Cancer

Great strength, even physical strength. The heavyweight. A music degree. Usually lucky with finances. Loneliness. "Alone again naturally." Fixed star Tejat.

Examples: actor Richard Boone (Pluto), businessman Sam Walton (Pluto), Lord Mountbatten, conductor Claudio Abbado, Francis I (Ascendant), athlete Willy Shoemaker (Ascendant), bank robber John Dillinger (Neptune), actor Cary Grant (Neptune), actor Douglas Fairbanks (Jupiter).

4 Cancer

A keen intuition. It is difficult to fool these people. The sixth sense. Music.

Examples: philosopher Michel de Montaigne (Saturn), conductor Toscanini (Uranus), aircraft designer/manufacturer Willy Messerschmitt.

5 Cancer

Some call this the miser's degree. These people have their fair share of emotional problems. Perhaps they are too judgmental. Maybe they're just sneaky. The right hand knows not what the left is doing.

Examples: composer Richard Rodgers, author Pearl S. Buck, politician Ferdinand Marcos (Pluto).

6 Cancer

People with this degree come on very strong. They have a high opinion of themselves, sometimes rightfully so. Still, their bragging is annoying. The boaster.

Examples: author Luigi Pirandello, author-activist Helen Keller, philosopher Jean-Jacques Rousseau, politician Pierre Laval, actress Kathy Bates.

7 Cancer

A bizarre but piquant imagination. The "Little Prince" mentality. There is often real strength here, too. A writer's degree.

Examples: author Saint-Exupery, author Shakespeare (Mars), author Honore de Balzac (Mars), artist Eugene Delacroix (Saturn), playwright George Bernard Shaw (Saturn), author D. H. Lawrence (Saturn), artist Peter Paul Rubens (Neptune), author Christopher Isherwood (Neptune), author William Faulkner (Ascendant), physician William Mayo, actor Slim Pickens, actor Gary Busey.

8 Cancer

A journalist's degree. Something peculiar or eccentric in the character. Otherwise they are perfectly harmless. And they are great gossips! The tell-tale.

Examples: publisher Larry Flynt (Ascendant), director William Wyler, actress Olivia de Havilland, singer Lena Horne, actress Karen Black.

9 Cancer

The luckiest degree in the zodiac! The pot of gold at the end of the rainbow. Money and the nice things of life keep pouring in. They end up as parents or in the public eye or both. And they take sincere enjoyment of their own good luck.

Examples: author Michel de Montaigne (Uranus), Baron von Rothchild, U.S. President Thomas Jefferson (Neptune), industrialist Howard Hughes (Neptune), industrialist Leland Stanford (Moon) actor Robert Stack (Jupiter), Prince Rainier (Pluto), actress Zsa Zsa Gabor (Pluto), politician Imelda Marcos, author George Sand, fashion designer Pierre Cardin (Sun and Pluto), Princess Diana, actress Leslie Caron, Queen Marie Antoinette

(Ascendant), singer Cher (Ascendant), director Sydney Pollack, athlete Carl Lewis, actress Liv Tyler, philosopher Liebniz.

10 Cancer

Strong attachment to home and family, the basic Cancer traits. Good memories. The homebody.

Examples: author Herman Hesse, actor George Sanders.

11 Cancer

Genius area of Cancer. Capable of deep research. The historian. Phenomenal memories. Can make a writer.

Examples: seer Nostradamus (Jupiter), mathematician Albert Einstein (Ascendant), marine biologist Rachel Carson (Jupiter and Neptune), Theosophist Alice Bailey (Mercury), author Franz Kafka, poet William Blake (Moon), and author Joseph Conrad (Moon), composer Igor Stravinsky (Mercury), military leader Giuseppe Garibaldi, actress Gina Lollobrigida.

12 Cancer

The businesslike and money-making side of Cancer gets started here and extends to the next four degrees, probably the influence of the Scorpio decanate. Nevertheless, these people must work hard for their money. They are creatures of habit. A degree of study and knowledge. The archivist.

Examples: scientist Madame Curie (Uranus), political theorist Hannah Arendt (Neptune), astrologer Robert Hand (Ascendant), U.S. President Calvin Coolidge, author Nathaniel Hawthorne, composer Stephen Foster, entertainer P. T. Barnum, entertainer Tokyo Rose, politician Henry Cabot Lodge, actress Eva Marie Saint, Dalai Lama.

13 Cancer

A sharp mind and a strong thirst for knowledge. Good teachers.

A business area. They have great energy. The financier. Fame, honor, or high office. Fixed star Sirius. However, they are perfectionists and often overly critical.

Examples: psychiatrist Carl Jung (Mercury), businessman Cecil Rhodes, businessman Alfried von Krupp (Neptune), businessman Lee Iacocca (Pluto), Emperor Maximilian, U.S. President George W. Bush, entertainer Merv Griffin, artist Frida Kahlo, author Jean Cocteau, businesswoman Nicky Hilton, actress Janet Leigh, singer Della Reese, actress Eva Green, Tolstoy (Ascendant).

14 Cancer

Lucky with the money. The golden touch. But a very highstrung degree. Mathematics.

Examples: author Mark Twain (Jupiter), bank robber Jesse James (Jupiter), athlete Jack Dempsey (Jupiter), U.S. Vice President Nelson Rockefeller (Neptune), singer Frank Sinatra (Saturn), comedian Bob Hope (Moon), entertainer Johnny Carson (Pluto), King Henry VIII, artist Felicien Rops, director Vittorio De Sica, historian Marc Bloch, musician Ringo Starr, First Lady Nancy Reagan, actor Sylvester Stallone.

15 Cancer

Also connected with money. They are attracted to meaningless titles. The hypocrite. Mathematics or economics. Nevertheless, this is one of the most powerful areas of Cancer, located in the center of the sign.

Examples: Count Ferdinand von Zeppelin, composer Gustav Mahler, artist Marc Chagall, author Elisabeth Kubler-Ross, politician Oliver Cromwell (Jupiter), industrialist Andrew Carnegie (Jupiter), businessman Jay Gould (Jupiter), actress Rita Hayworth (Jupiter), actress Olivia de Havilland (Moon).

16 Cancer

The last degree of the Cancer money and business area. They are brave, intelligent, but can also be dishonest. The con man.

Examples: industrialist John D. Rockefeller, U.S. Vice President Nelson Rockerfeller, artist Peter Paul Rubens, psychologist Alfred Binet, athlete O.J. Simpson, composer Ottorino Respighi, actress Anjelica Huston, politician Joseph McCarthy (Neptune), murderer David Berkowitz (Uranus).

17 Cancer

Intelligent. A desire to travel. But they are somehow limited. Hamlet: "Oh God, I could be bounded in a nutshell." Nervous or unstable.

Examples: author Barabara Cartland, inventor Nikola Tesla, composer Carl Orff, musician Arlo Guthrie, journalist David Brinkley, politician Donald Rumsfeld, actor Tom Hanks, actress Courtney Love.

18 Cancer

The juvenile delinquent. This degree is considered rather anti-social. They don't want to go along with the program. Sometimes connected to violence. Fixed star Wasat. Perhaps they are merely frustrated.

Examples: author Marcel Proust, playwright George Bernard Shaw (Mercury), artist Whistler (Sun and Mercury), revolutionary Vladimir Lenin (Uranus), gangster Leggs Diamond, actor Yul Brynner, singer Hermann Prey.

19 Cancer

This degree is interested in education. Therefore they make good teachers. But we also find many artists here. The educator.

Examples: occultist H. P. Blavatsky (Ascendant), First Lady Eleanor Roosevelt (Moon), U.S. President Lyndon B. Johnson (Venus), artist Andrew Wyeth, pianist Van Cliburn, actor Milton Berle, actor Bill Cosby.

20 Cancer

This degree is weaker than most in Cancer. Nevertheless, the mind is intelligent. Sometimes an artistic influence. Yet they are also limited. Glorious defeat. They often end up as slaves to the family.

Examples: author David Henry Thoreau, artist Amedeo Modiliani, entertainer Dave Garroway, actor Harrison Ford.

21 Cancer

This is also a weak degree. They have a rebellious streak and prize their freedom very highly. The free artist. Music

Examples: activist Jerry Rubin, director Ingmar Bergman, composer Claude Debussy (Moon), actress Cameron Diaz (Moon), U.S. President Gerald Ford, author Iris Murdock, actress Polly Bergen.

22 Cancer

This is a strong painter's degree, and Cancer produces many aritsts. It creates many unique individuals and possibly a genius. A strong degree for women. The painter.

Examples: artist Rembrandt, artist Leonardo da Vinci (Uranus), artist Salvador Dali (Ascendant), artist Jackson Pollock (Neptune), activist Emmaline Pankhurst, actress Barbara Stanwyck, dancer Ginger Rogers, singer Linda Ronstadt, actress Brigitte Nielsen.

23 Cancer

This is the "rising up the ladder of success" degree. Most of these people manage to get ahead in their careers.

Examples: Alexander the Great, theologian Mary Baker Eddy,

Queen Elizabeth I (Saturn), German President Paul von Hindenburg (Moon), physicist R. J. Oppenheimer (Moon), fashion designer Coco Chanel (Jupiter), athlete Joe Namath (Jupiter), athlete Rocky Marciano (Venus), Duchess Camilla Parker Bowles.

24 Cancer

A very powerful and successful degree. Some rise like a meteor. They must learn gentleness and compassion. The success story.

Examples: actor James Cagney, actor Donald Sutherland, author James Thackeray, artist Jean-Baptiste Corot, physician-educator Maria Montessori (Mars and Uranus), explorer Roald Amundsen (Sun and Venus), dictator Fidel Castro (Venus), singer Bing Crosby (Moon), entertainer Art Linkletter, comedian Phyllis Diller, singer Jimi Hendrix (Jupiter), author Stephen King (Mars), singer Phoebe Snow, politician Angela Merkel.

25 Cancer

This is a degree that indicates success and confidence. Preferment can come quite suddenly. Overnight fame. Fixed star Procyon. Great courage resides here. Also writing talent.

Examples: Emperor Napoleon (Saturn) and actress Charlize Theron (Saturn), Lord Byron (Moon), astronaut John Glenn, actor Steve McQueen (Ascendant), comedian Red Skelton (Sun and Neptune), actor Vin Diesel, poet Yevgeny Yevtushenko.

26 Cancer

Another painting degree. Often poetic or artistic. It seems also to produce a lot of farmers. The agriculturist.

Examples: artist Van Dyck (Ascendant), artist Edward Degas, author Johann Goethe (Neptune), art critic John Ruskin (Moon), author Pearl Buck (Moon), author Marcel Proust (Uranus), author Herman Hesse (Venus), author A. J. Cronin, Sir Edmund Hillary, physician Charles Mayo, singer Carlos Santana, actress Diana Rigg.

27 Cancer

Interested in the spiritual or occult side of life. The mystic. Perhaps religion. It has an artistic influence as well.

Examples: theologian John Calvin, author Joseph Conrad (Saturn), actress Natalie Wood, actress Julia Roberts (Ascendant), murderer Lizzie Borden, singer Kim Carnes.

28 Cancer

The last two degrees of Cancer are generally rather weak. They produce a lot of large children. Perhaps this is the influence of the Leo cusp coming in. Cautious. "Suspicion torments my heart, suspicion keeps us apart."

Examples: philosopher Count Keyserling, author Ernest Hemingway, actor Terence Stamp, actor Robin Williams, singer Cat Stevens, actress Angelina Jolie (Ascendant and Venus).

29 Cancer

Many children. They have a hard time taking care of themselves or knowing what to do. They are not stupid, merely indecisive and unpredictable. Sensitive, impressionable. Must be handled with kid gloves.

Examples: astronomer-astrologer John Dee, murderer Myra Hindley, poet Hart Crane, Emperor Haile Selassie, singer George Clinton, actor Willem Dafoe.

Leo

0 Leo

The first two degrees of Leo come in roaring like a lion, but actually they are pussy-cats underneath. Yet there is a certain blunt honesty. They are of course also proud, if not altogether arrogant.

Examples: White House intern Monica Lewinsky, comedian David Spade, philanthropist Rose Kennedy, author Alexandre Dumas, poet Robert Graves, author Raymond Chandler, athlete Don Drysdale, director Theo Van Gogh.

1 Leo

Still a lot of huffing and puffing going on here. The mouse that roars. They put up a good front but are less sure of themselves than they appear. Something gentle underneath however.

Examples: philosopher Omar Khayyam, author Zelda Fitzgerald.

2 Leo

At this degree, Leo starts to become the leader. They have sharp minds and can easily explain things. Thus they make good teachers. A big ego.

Examples: author James Joyce (Moon), aviator Amelia Earhart, actor Jason Robards, actress Helen Mirren, actress Heather Locklear, musician Mick Jagger.

3 Leo

An intellectual degree. A penetrating and analytical mind, capable of profound research. Honest, sincere. A writing degree. The researcher.

Examples: author Aldous Huxley, mathematician-inventor Blaise Pascal (Saturn), psychiatrist Carl Jung, artist Joshua Reynolds, playwright George Bernard Shaw, author Andre Maurois, author Pearl S. Buck (Moon), director Stanley Kubrick.

4 Leo

Diogenes with his lamp at last discovers an honest man. This degree is as solid as a rock. They have their feet on the ground. Integrity. You can count on them when the chips are down. Excellent researchers but business is also a possibility.

Examples: scholar Francesco Petrarch, author Hilaire Belloc. playwright George Bernard Shaw (Venus), philanthropist Lillian Carter (Moon), U.S. Vice President Al Gore (Ascendant), astrologer Liz Greene (Saturn), Walter Cronkite (Neptune).

5 Leo

There is a strong militant nature to this degree. They make good military leaders. They are extremely active and must learn to control their passions; otherwise they can experience a lot of pain and trouble. The militarist.

Examples: political thinker-historian Alexis de Tocqueville, athlete Vida Blue, First Lady Jacqueline Kennedy, businessman Cecil Rhodes (Mercury), dictator Benito Mussolini (Mercury), actor George C. Scott (Moon), athlete Joe Louis (Mars), artist Pablo Picasso (Ascendant), politician Juan Peron (Jupiter), poet Gerard Manley Hopkins, artist Marcel Duchamp, Prince Aly Khan (Venus).

6 Leo

The dictator. Often a military degree. This degree is very powerful and quite frequently successful. They have big plans. Unfortunately they are also extremely arrogant and always trying to be the leader of the pack, the chief actor on the stage. They need a great deal of attention.

Examples: dictator Benito Mussolini, military leader Chiang Kai-shek (Saturn), industrialist Henry Ford (Mercury), King Henry VIII (Mercury), theologian John Calvin (Mercury), Emperor Napoleon (Mercury), murderer Heinrich Himmler (Mars), military leader Ernst Roehm (Saturn), author Emily Bronte, actress Clara Bow, actor Louis de Funes, actor-politician Arnold Schwarzenegger, entertainer Harry Houdini (Uranus), poet Robert Frost (Uranus), artist Andy Warhol (Venus), author Jean Genet (Moon), singer Diana Ross (Pluto), musician Mick Jagger (Pluto), actor Jean Reno, actress Lisa Kudrow.

7 Leo

The lottery winner. A very fortunate financial degree. There are many positive virtues incorporated here and these natives tend to succeed in any direction in which they go.

Examples: athlete Willy Shoemaker (Jupiter), actor James Stewart (Jupiter), athlete Jean-Claude Killy (Pluto), fashion designer Calvin Klein (Pluto), publisher Larry Flynt (Pluto), businessman Sam Walton (Saturn), model Twiggy (Moon and Mars), U.S. President George W. Bush (Ascendant), sculptor Henry Moore.

8 Leo

There are many positive influences here as well. However they do seem to be difficult to understand. An enigma. It appears to make a good writer of sea tales.

Examples: author Herman Melville, author Richard Henry Dana, actress Geraldine Chaplin.

9 Leo

An interest in the occult or mystical. Perhaps sales. Some artistic influence. Or someone busy with fashion. The king of fashion.

Examples: Composer Francis Scott Key, actor Peter O'Toole, fashion designer Yves Saint Laurant, businesswoman Paris Hilton (Moon).

10 Leo

These people seem to have a lot of emotional difficulties and issues in their relationships. Perhaps they must simply learn to become more honest. Out of sight, out of mind. Nevertheless, they have a pleasant exterior.

Examples: Actress Myna Loy, actress Dolores del Rio, singer Tony Bennett, singer Barbara Streisand (Moon), media mogul Martha Stewart.

11 Leo

An occult influence of one sort or another. These people might be good astrologers, or just sail off to the moon. The dreamer. There is also gentleness here. Something charming. Lucky with money, particularly with partners.

Examples: fashion designer Louis Vuitton, heiress Cornelia Vanderbilt (Mercury), musician Paul McCartney (Moon), poet Rupert Brooke, actor Ernie Pyle, Robert Taylor, actor Martin Sheen, choreographer Rudi Dantzig.

12 Leo

This is another lucky money degree. Besides that, there is something resembling pure joy in this degree. They are fun to be around, a comfort to everyone. The idealist. This degree brings in the artist's feeling for beauty.

Examples: author Guy de Maupassant, musician Louis Armstrong, director John Huston, astronaut Neil Armstrong,

U.S. President Barack Obama, astrologer Sydney Omarr, singer Peggy Lee (Jupiter), actor Johnny Depp (Ascendant), poet Shelley (Venus), songwriter Stephen Foster (Venus), poet Yeats (Mars).

13 Leo

This degree is associated with poets. There is a great appreciation for beauty. These people are very social; they like to party. They need to let off steam once in a while. But there is a stubborn and deeply egotistical side to the character as well. Selfish little pig.

Examples: poet Shelley, poet Tennyson, poet Ronsard (Mars), poet Paul Claudel, poet Yevtushenko (Mercury), actress Lucille Ball, artist Andy Warhol, actress Jane Fonda (Ascendant), singer Cher (Mars), dictator Adolf Hitler (Saturn), actor Charlie Chaplin (Saturn), Sir Alexander Fleming, actor Robert Mitchum, author Jack Kerouac (Neptune), singer Michael Jackson (Uranus).

14 Leo

The feeling for art and beauty continues with this degree, as well as the desire sometimes to celebrate through the night. The party-man. Often music. Many good ideas. But they must learn to keep their feet on the ground.

Examples: astrologer Alan Leo, producer Dino De Laurentiis.

15 Leo

A strong degree with some of the best Leo characteristics: straightforward, warm-hearted, and noble. This is also a powerful and creative degree. They generally achieve their goals. There is curiosity here, including the occult. "Now cracks a noble heart."—Hamlet

Examples: author Oscar Wilde (Moon), dancer Mata Hari, actor Rory Calhoun, athlete Esther Williams.

16 Leo

Peter Pan. A very childish degree. They seem to refuse to grow up. They are like actors going out on the stage for the first time. Somehow weird or peculiar.

Examples: comedian Phyllis Diller (Venus), psychologist Jean Piaget, actor Dustin Hoffman, singer Whitney Houston, politician Romano Prodi.

17 Leo

People with this degree like to do everything their own way. They're also intelligent, but too critical. Rough or uncouth. Grateful and generous, but also capable of revenge. The avenger.

Examples: professional assassin Carlos the Jackal (Pluto), actress Norma Shearer, singer Eddie Fisher, actress Melanie Griffith.

18 Leo

This degree gives the appearance of great strength and is perhaps very spiritual. The new messiah?

Examples: Poet Shelley (Uranus), U.S. President Herbert Hoover, Theosophist Madame Blavatsky, author Alex Haley, astrologer Robert de Luce (Ascendant), actor Antonio Banderas, engineer Steve Wozniak.

19 Leo

Weaker than most Leo degrees. The occult. An entertainer.

Examples: poet Robert Southey, businessman Alfred von Krupp, director Cecil B. DeMille.

20 Leo

This is also one of the weaker degrees. There is something demanding or frustrating. However, Leo's feeling for entertainment is continuing in this degree. Especially the movies. The film producer.

Examples: director Alfred Hitchcock, director Cecil B. DeMille (Ascendant), actress Shelley Long (Moon), actress Greta Garbo (Venus), businessman Diamond Jim Brady, politician John Dean.

21 Leo

This is a very sympathetic degree of Leo. These people have a calming effect upon others. The pacifier. There is a keen intuition here and they make excellent doctors.

Examples: psychic Edgar Cayce (Uranus), author John Galsworthy, actor Steve Martin, actress Halle Berry.

22 Leo

This is a powerful degree. These people are strong leaders and wonderful entertainers. They especially make great clowns. Also a medical area. Let me entertain you.

Examples: Emperor Napoleon, Emperor Franz Joseph (Moon and Saturn), revolutionary Leon Trotsky (Moon), entertainer Ed Sullivan (Moon), singer Birgit Nilsson (Moon), actress Ethel Barrymore, composer Claude Debussy (Ascendant), politician Jawaharlal Nehru (Ascendant), military leader T. E. Lawrence (Ascendant), politician Menachem Begin, Princess Anne, Queen Elizabeth II (Neptune), actor Rod Serling (Neptune), entertainer Jerry Lewis (Neptune), musician Miles Davis (Neptune), actress Marilyn Monroe (Neptune), musician Nat King Cole (Saturn), singer Natalie Wood (Mercury), actor Ben Affleck, Sir Walter Scott, philanthropist Lillian Carter.

23 Leo

This is a degree of intellectual genius perhaps equal to the opposite degree in Aquarius. Actors. Physicians. The universal genius.

Examples: physician Wilhelm Wundt, author Norman Mahler (Saturn), physician Anton Chekov (Saturn), military leader T.E.

Lawrence, poet Ted Hughes, chef Julia Child, actor Peter Sellers (Neptune), actor Robert Culp, actor Robert DeNiro, singer Madonna.

24 Leo

A very sweet degree. Many are outstanding mothers. They love to take care of and protect anything young and defenseless. Almost big children themselves.

Examples: Emperor Franz Joseph, explorer Davy Crockett, actress Shelley Winters, astrologer-publisher Llewellyn George, director Roman Polanski, First Lady Rosalynn Carter, athlete Rafer Johnson, actress Julia Roberts (Moon), actor Sean Penn, "Mom."

25 Leo

Often called "the great lover" degree. It is matched only by the opposite degree in Aquarius, which has the same influence. It sometimes produces women of loose morals. At any rate, these people especially love to enjoy themselves.

Examples: Comtesse Madame du Barry, singer Enrico Caruso (Jupiter), actress Rita Hayworth (Saturn), actor Robert Redford, actor Patrick Swayze, conductor Antonio Salieri, athlete Willy Shoemaker, poet Ogden Nash, actor Edward Norton, actress Mae West.

26 Leo

Another astrology area begins in this degree and carries on for the rest of the sign. There is intelligence here, but on the whole it is a dull and uninteresting degree. Conservative in nature. Attention to detail. A bore.

Examples: poet John Dryden, aviator Orville Wright, fashion designer Coco Chanel, philosopher Paul Tillich, actress Jill St. John, financier Bernard Baruch, singer Elizabeth Schwarzkopf (Mars), U.S. President Bill Clinton, musician Issac Hayes, actor Matthew Perry.

27 Leo

Has many good ideas. However, people with this degree are impatient and very quickly reap what they sow. Their karma bounces back at them. They should try to slow down. Karmic payback. Nemesis.

Examples: U.S. Vice President Spiro Agnew (Saturn), author Jacqueline Susann, politician Slobodan Milosevic.

28 Leo

These people are idealistic and very keen on friendship and group activities, which is more a trait of Aquarius than Leo. They want to cooperate and share. The faithful friend. A ladies man. They are also lucky with the money. A musical degree.

Examples: Illustrator-author Aubrey Beardsley, athlete Wilt Chamberlain, entrepreneur Bill Gates (Pluto), composer Anton Bruckner (Ascendant), composer Claude Debussy, politician Deng Xiaoping, musician John Lee Hooker.

29 Leo

This degree produces leaders. The king. Fixed star Regulus. They have willpower and determination, but this seems odd because the cusp of Virgo is about to begin.

Examples: Mary, Queen of Scots (Uranus), King Louis XVI (Sun and Jupiter), U.S. President Thomas Jefferson (Saturn), revolutionary Toussaint L'Ouverture (Saturn), composer Franz Liszt (Ascendant), poet Walt Whitman (Moon), politician Winston Churchill (Moon), heiress Cornelia Vanderbilt, author Ray Bradbury (Sun and Jupiter), dancer Gene Kelly, actress Shelley Long.

Virgo

0 Virgo

The king versus the servant. There is a sort of war of the cusps (Leo versus Virgo) going on in this degree and some lesson in humility to be learned.

Examples: Poet Dorothy Parker, author Jorge Luis Borges.

1 Virgo

This degree indicates a strategist. Also, they are the life of the party and enjoy being the center of attention, so there is something of Leo left over here. "The most popular student in the class." Music. A clear and orderly mind.

Examples: Actor Sean Connery, actor Peter O'Toole (Mercury), military leader George S. Patton (Mars), Princess Diana (Mars), politician Silvio Berlusconi (Mars), actress Julia Roberts (Jupiter), singer Madonna (Pluto), conductor Leonard Berstein, musician Leo Ferre, physician-scientist Hans Adolf Krebs, astrologer Robert de Luce, author Bret Harte, politician George Wallace.

2 Virgo

The computer brain. The minds of people with this degree work quickly and efficiently, making all the necessary calculations. This is a good writer's degree. "Analyze all things."—Marcus Aurelius

Examples: astronomer Nicolaus Copernicus (Ascendant), politician Dick Cheney (Ascendant), actress Shelley Long (ascendant), philosopher Rene Descartes (Saturn), Baron Rothschild (Saturn), comedian Lenny Bruce (Moon), Prince Albert.

3 Virgo

This is most likely the luckiest degree in Virgo, which can also be said for the opposite degree in Pisces. Lady Luck. Makes a good employee.

Examples: media mogul Rupert Murdoch (Neptune), musician John Lennon (Venus), author Theodore Dreiser, U.S. President Lyndon Baines Johnson, producer Samuel Goldwyn, poet Guillaume Apollinaire, novelist Christopher Isherwood, politician Yasser Arafat, actress Tuesday Weld, singer Lisa Marie Presley (Jupiter), astrologer Zipporah Dobyns.

4 Virgo

The Aquarian Age. A very enlightened degree in Virgo. Ready and willing to help others. Perhaps a degree of genius.

Examples: philosopher Georg Hegel, U.S. President Thomas Jefferson (Jupiter), actor Ben Gazzara, actor David Soul, author D. H. Lawrence (Mercury), astrologer R. C. Jansky (Moon), politician Lech Walesa (Venus), singer Bob Geldof (Venus), fashion designer Don Loper, actress Ingrid Bergman, singer Tommy Sands.

5 Virgo

People with this degree are usually excellent employees. Very Virgo in its essence. Practical and down-to-earth.

Examples: author Johann Goethe, author Maurice Maeterlinck, conductor Karl Bohm, actor Charles Boyer, actor Elliott Gould, athlete Jean-Claude Killy, singer Michael Jackson.

6 Virgo

People with this degree are capable of regenerating themselves. And, indeed, they are very often in need of regeneration. The drug addict. There is a tendency simply to enjoy themselves and take the easy path.

Examples: politician Edward Kennedy (Moon and Neptune), entertainer Dick Gregory (Venus) comedian Chevy Chase (Venus), singer Johnny Cash (Neptune), actor Larry Hagman (Neptune), politician Eldridge Cleaver, Emperor Caligula, King Henry VIII (Ascendant), athlete Ted Williams, politician John McCain.

7 Virgo

The old maid degree. In general very often shy and prudish. They have however basically an honest and moral character. Focus on diet. Can be a good astrology student.

Examples: author Mary Shelley, educator Maria Montessori, politician Huey P. Long, comedian Lily Tomlin, actor Timothy Bottoms, actress Cameron Diaz, actress Greta Garbo (Mercury), and actress Dolores del Rio (Mercury).

8 Virgo

These people have good hearts but are somehow naive. A simple soul.

Examples: Queen Wilhelmina, actor Fredric March, athlete Rocky Marciano, actor James Coburn, author William Saroyan, singer Van Morrison.

9 Virgo

This degree is a little bit too humble. Models. But there can also be an aggressive streak associated with this degree. They tend to have a fatalistic philosophy. The Ides of March. There is an interest in the occult and the mysteries of the universe.

Examples: actress Lucille Ball (Mercury), actress Kim Novak (Neptune), actress Jennifer Beals (Uranus), Ivan the Terrible (Mars), murderer Dan White, athlete James Corbett, actor Keanu Reeves (Sun and Mercury), media personality Dr. Phil, actor Mark Harmon.

10 Virgo

This is an astrology degree. This is a very straightforward and practical degree of Virgo. These people are self-sufficient, they can take care of themselves. The independent one.

Examples: politician Jean Jaures.

11 Virgo

Another astrology degree. Or interest in the mystical. The occultist. But here we also have an artistic side of Virgo making its appearance. On the other hand, there may be a violent side to this degree. The wife-beater.

Examples: Psychic Elsie Wheeler, astrologer-author Liz Greene, activist Timothy Leary (Jupiter), composer Anton Bruckner, architect Louis H. Sullivan, Ivan the Terrible, bank robber Jesse James, gangster Mickey Cohen, Lucrezia Borgia (Saturn), actor Charlie Sheen.

12 Virgo

There is something romantic and poetic about this degree. The imaginative artist. There may also be ability for music. They love animals. Sometimes overly interested in sex.

Examples: poet Samuel Coleridge (Venus), author Arthur Koestler, composer Mozart (Ascendant), singer Peggy Lee (Ascendant), composer John Cage, musician Leonard Cohen (Venus and Neptune). singer Beyonce, actress Brigitte Bardot (Neptune), King Louis XIV, businessman Jack Valenti, politician Paul Volcker.

13 Virgo

This degree is artistic but also has its business side, as it is in the Capricorn decanate of Virgo. They are hard-working and industrious. There is a certain reserve and quiet calmness here. "Hence, in being content, one will always have enough."—Lao Tzu.

Examples: politician Lafayette, social worker Jane Addams, actress Raquel Welch, actor Peter Lawford.

14 Virgo

These people are very hard-working, especially regarding paperwork. The desk worker. It is a good business area. A degree of change and transformation. It seems to also produce actors.

Examples: author Lewis Carroll (Saturn), author Taylor Caldwell, politician Paul Volcker (Mercury), businessman Joe Kennedy, impresario Billy Rose, musician Chrissie Hynde.

15 Virgo

One of the most beautiful degrees of Virgo. Sweet, loving, and always helpful. It is a lovely degree for women. The sweet sister. They are intelligent and mostly successful.

Examples: composer Anton Dvorak, author Frederic Mistral, artist Grandma Moses, author James Hilton, musician Buddy Holly, actor Peter Sellers.

16 Virgo

The salt of the earth degree. Very dependable people. They make the best of friends. Hard workers. It can also make a philosopher.

Examples: Theologian Cardinal Richelieu, philosopher John Locke, singer Patsy Cline.

17 Virgo

These people have less integrity and tend to take advantage of the situation. It can make for a very devious politician. The demagogue, the rabble rouser. Also a writing degree.

Examples: U.S. President Andrew Jackson (Jupiter), U.S. President Franklin Delano Roosevelt's (Uranus), U.S. President Richard Nixon (Ascendant), religious leader Khomeini (Ascendant), publisher William Randolph Hearst (Moon), murderer Bruno Hauptmann (Moon), U.S. President John Kennedy (Moon), author John Milton (Neptune), politician Silvio Berlusconi (Neptune), politician Ferdinand Marcos, author Leo Tolstoy, author Jessica Mitford, athlete Roger Maris, singer Jose Feliciano.

18 Virgo

Another sweet degree in Virgo. They take care of anything small and innocent. The protector. This is a strong writing area in Virgo.

Examples: actress Julia Roberts (Venus), author Charles Dickens (Ascendant), author D. H. Lawrence, author William Saroyan (Mercury).

19 Virgo

Writing talent. But there is in addition something very strong and courageous in this degree. They are rough and ready, and also thinkers. The rugged individualist. Maybe music.

Examples: author Friedrich Engels (Moon), author Emily Dickinson (Ascendant), short story writer O. Henry, poet John Dryden (Uranus), economist John Maynard Keynes (Uranus), author Franz Kafka (Uranus), author H. G. Wells (Mercury), poet Ted Hughes (Mercury), poet Yevgeny Yevtushenko (Jupiter), actress Claudette Colbert, director Brian De Palma, actor Maurice Chevalier, singer Barry White.

20 Virgo

Music and writing. Also more bravery. These people never back down in the face of a challenge. Intestinal fortitude.

Examples: composer Arnold Schoenberg, author Roald Dahl, author H. L. Mencken, author J. B. Priestley, composer Maurice Jarre, musician Clara Schumann, explorer Davy Crockett (Mars), author Ernest Hemingway (Mars), singer Nina Simone (Jupiter), athlete Serena Williams (Moon).

21 Virgo

The penny-pincher. They say this degree makes a cheapskate. And that is sometimes true. But it is also gives a good brain and an excellent memory.

Examples: artist Michelangelo (Pluto), singer Amy Winehouse.

22 Virgo

This degree gets along well with the group. Hail fellow, well met. Also makes a good friend. The all-round "good guy." An artistic side of Virgo is coming in again, but especially writers because this is Virgo's strong point.

Examples: author Agatha Christie, author Sherwood Anderson, director Oliver Stone (Sun and Mercury), actor Jackie Cooper, actor Tommy Lee Jones.

23 Virgo

Artists, especially actors. The femme fatale. These people are restless.

Examples: actress Anne Bancroft, actress Lauren Bacall, politician Robert Dudley, dancer George Chakiris, actress Gene Tierny (Saturn), actress Lana Turner (Saturn), dancer Gene Kelly (Mars), actress Lillian Gish (Ascendant), model Brooke Shields (Ascendant), actress Lucille Ball (Venus), actress Liv Ullman (Neptune), actor Al Pacino (Neptune), Paul Hogan

(Neptune), U.S. President William Taft, author James Fenimore Cooper, singer Hank Williams, entertainer David Copperfield.

24 Virgo

This degree is generally weak. But not always. The virgin queen. There seems to be some artistic ability. Good with patterns and colors. Often musical or mystical or both. Perhaps they are lonelier than others.

Examples: Queen Elizabeth I, actor Roddy McDowall.

25 Virgo

Virgo starts to become literary again in this degree. There is something mysterious about these natives. The vamp. Sex appeal and a big sense of humor.

Examples: author Samuel Johnson, author William Golding. author George Orwell (Ascendant), poet Robert Frost (Jupiter), actress Greta Garbo, actress Frances Farmer, singer Fanny Brice (Saturn), actor Ted Danson (Ascendant), actress Julie Christie (Neptune), singer Kylie Minoque (Uranus), actress Catherine Zeta-Jones (Pluto), actress Jennifer Lopez (Pluto), singer Jessye Norman, model Twiggy.

26 Virgo

Literature. The novelist. Philosophy is also favored. There is intelligence and a basic honesty.

Examples: author Italo Svevo (Jupiter), author William Faulkner (Mercury), author Johann Goethe (Venus), actress Sophia Loren, singer Cass Elliot.

27 Virgo

This degree can produce very mental types. The classical egghead. But also a leader or a businessperson. Writers. Music. Some interest in astrology.

Examples: scientist Antonie van Leeuwenhoek (Uranus), architect Christopher Wren (Uranus), author Samuel Johnson (Mercury), author Ezra Pound (Jupiter), Emperor Augustus Caesar, military leader Rommel (Saturn), athlete Arnold Palmer, terrorist Osama bin Laden (Jupiter), author Ronsard, author Upton Sinclair, author Stephen King, author Nietzsche (Mars), composer Igor Stravinsky (Ascendant), singer Leonard Cohen (Sun and Ascendant), astrologer Robert de Luce (Mercury), actor Larry Hagman.

28 Virgo

This degree can be associated with astrologers. There is a desire to help humanity. The well-wisher. Sometimes a writer. In general intelligent and active.

Examples: author H. G. Wells, author Fay Weldon, author William Faulkner (Moon), composer Gustav Holst, King Francis I.

29 Virgo

These people often like to collect things, and seem to be tied down by one thing or another. Perhaps even by a partner or children. The collector.

Examples: publisher William Randolph Hearst (Saturn), politician Aldo Moro, musician Julio Iglesias.

Libra

0 Libra

Libra comes in with a large ego equal to the size of Aries. There is also a clear sharp intelligence in this degree. However they do not get along well with partners, perhaps due to selfishness. They often end up alone. Melancholy. The lonely one.

Examples: military leader Albrecht von Wallenstein, politician Sir William Cecil, artist Suzanne Valadon, poet Dorothy Parker (Venus), actress Romy Schneider (Sun and Moon), actor Mickey Rooney, musician John Coltrane, singer Bruce Springsteen.

1 Libra

Both the intelligence and the loneliness continues. The self-kicker. They are very busy with themselves. Very honest and with good intentions, but somehow they appear rigid and critical. A sad note, too. Music.

Examples: director Ingmar Bergman (Moon), composer Dmitri Shostakovitch, musician Linda McCartney, artist Paul Delvaux, journalist Barbara Walters, journalist Jim McKay.

2 Libra

A musical degree. Writers. Here we find all the refined sensitivity of the creative artist. The aesthete. Also something pessimistic.

Examples: author F. Scott Fitzgerald, actress Catherine Deneuve (Neptune), model Cheryl Tiegs, musician Bryan Ferry, actor Christopher Reeve (Sun and Mercury), actor Michael Douglas, actress Catherine Zeta-Jones, actress Heather Locklear, actor Will Smith.

3 Libra

Music. There is refinement in this degree but there is also something stiff and unapproachable about them. Rather severe types. A womanizer.

Examples: composer George Gershwin, conductor Charles Munch, musician Nat King Cole (Moon), singer Olivia Newton-John, singer Meat Loaf, actress Britney Spears (Ascendant), author T.S. Eliot, author William Faulkner, philosopher Martin Heidegger, actor Marcello Mastroianni, philosopher Bertrand Russell (Moon), musician Louis Armstrong (Moon), athlete Serena Williams.

4 Libra

This is the degree of the ultra-conservative. Intellectual and fussy. However, they often miss opportunities and should raise their opinion of themselves. An inferiority complex.

Examples: entertainer Ed Sullivan, actress Brigitte Bardot, commentator Barbara Walters (Ascendant), scientist Alfred Nobel (Saturn), author Prosper Merimee, athlete Max Schmeling, actress Gwyneth Paltrow.

5 Libra

This is sometimes a cruel degree, and these people can be intense. The sadist. They also have a special problem with communication that can be painful for them.

Examples: military leader Henri Petain's Mars, politician Georges Clemenceau, actor Peter Finch, singer Jerry Lee Lewis, politician Lech Walesa, politician Silvio Berlusconi.

6 Libra

Dancers. A love of danger. The dare-devil. Something fated about the destiny course of this degree. A child of fate. They love birds.

Examples: military leader Horatio Nelson, poet Arthur Rimbaud (Moon), actress Gloria Swanson (Moon), military leader George Patton (Uranus), murderer Marc Dutroux (Venus), author Unamuno de Jugo, artist Michaelangelo Antonioni, actress Deborah Kerr, singer Johnny Mathis, actress Angie Dickinson, political assassin Carlos the Jackal (Ascendant).

7 Libra

Dancers. Love of danger. And, for the rest, they are rather strange types. The eccentric.

Examples: bank robber Bonnie Parker, theologian Girolamo Savonarola, theosophist Annie Besant, composer Paul Dukas. author Truman Capote, actress Julie Andrews, actor Richard Harris.

8 Libra

There is something tragic about this degree. Sometimes scandal. They may lose their partners. The widow. Artistic and literary. There is also great courage.

Examples: author Sylvia Plath (Moon), playwright Oscar Wilde (Venus), athlete O. J. Simpson (Neptune), author George Orwell (Mars), musician Yoko Ono (Ascendant), actor Liam Neeson (Saturn), actor Graham Greene, author Faith Baldwin, politician Mohandas Gandhi, poliltican Paul von Hindenburg, astrologer-author Marc Edmund Jones, actor George Peppard, U.S. President Jimmy Carter, singer Sting.

9 Libra

Danger of tragedy and loss of partner. Fixed star Vindemiatrix. This is a strong literature area. The man or woman of letters.

They are charming and refined, yet on the other hand there is also a critical and fault-finding side to their nature. Music.

Examples: author Thomas Wolfe, poet Wallace Stevens, author Gore Vidal, author Nikolai Gogol (Moon), author Theodore Dreiser (Venus), poet e.e.cummings (Venus), painter Pierre Bonnard, actress Eleonora Duse, comedian Groucho Marx, military leader Ferdinand Foch (Sun and Venus).

10 Libra

This is one of the weaker degrees. Perhaps they don't try hard enough. A tendency to isolation. Child welfare. Sometimes hygiene. The social worker.

Examples: author Emily Post, actor Charlton Heston, actress Susan Sarandon.

11 Libra

The Dr. Jekyll and Mr. Hyde degree. They are quite intelligent and capable of being cruel. They work hard. Film actors.

Examples: U.S. President Rutherford B. Hayes, U.S. President Chester A. Arthur, financier Juan March, murderer Josef Mengele (Moon), politician Huey P. Long (Saturn), actor Buster Keaton, actress Natalie Wood (Ascendant), actor Kevin Kline (Neptune), singer Steve Miller, actress Alicia Silverstone, singer Bob Geldof.

12 Libra

A rather weak degree. More film actors. They seem somehow oblivious, can be slow learners, and lack confidence. Loneliness. The actress.

Examples: actress Britt Ekland, author Hans Christian Andersen (Saturn), author Thor Heyerdahl.

13 Libra

An acting degree. Not very lucky. Still, they are refined and gentle. Some may have emotional problems. The movie star.

Examples: singer Jenny Lind, actress Claudette Colbert (Ascendant), actor Paul Hogan, actress Carol Lombard, murderer Heinrich Himmler, militant Ulrike Meinhof, politician Vladimir Putin, King Louis Philippe I, psychiatrist R. D. Laing, industrialist George Westinghouse, arhitect Le Corbusier, astrologer Stephen Arroyo, military leader Oliver North.

14 Libra

Acting. But these people act so well they even fool themselves about who they are. The self-illusionist. Makes a good politician.

Examples: actress Rita Hayworth (Venus), actress Doris Day (Jupiter), comedian Chevy Chase, Esternado Waldo Demara (Jupiter), actor Rudolph Valentino (Moon), politician Juan Peron, scientist Neils Bohr.

15 Libra

An identity crisis. A musical area. Actors.

Examples: composer Modest Mussorgsky (Jupiter), composer Hector Berlioz (Uranus), composer Camille Saint-Saens, musician Chuck Berry (Venus), military leader Alfred Dreyfus, military leader Eddie Rickenbacker, sculptor Alberto Giacometti, U.S. Vice President Henry A. Wallace, activist Jesse Jackson, actress Sigourney Weaver, actor Matt Damon.

16 Libra

This degree indicates intelligence, energy, and hard-work, and is especially strong as an Ascendant degree. Ingenious, these people can be good astrologers and clever criminals. The mastermind.

Examples: author Ralph Waldo Emerson (Ascendant), astrologer C.E.O. Carter (Ascendant), bank robber Jesse James (Venus), author T.S. Eliot (Uranus), astrologer Liz Greene (Mars), actress Helen Hayes, playwright Harold Pinter, author James Clavell, musician John Lennon.

17 Libra

Another degree that often has criminal tendencies. Possible violence. There is passion here. And a great love of oratory or debate. The polemicist. They want to be the greatest. Also musical.

Examples: bank robber Billy the Kid (Mars), financier Juan March (Moon), poet Samuel Coleridge (Mercury), author Alexis de Tocqueville (Uranus), composer Verdi (Sun and Mercury), musician Thelonious Monk, singer Luciano Pavarotti.

18 Libra

This is most likely the most brilliant degree of Libra. They are intellectual and artistic. Often makes a writer. The man of reason. Very hospitable.

Examples: First Lady Eleanor Roosevelt, physicist Sir Isaac Newton (Ascendant), composer Johann Sebastian Bach (Jupiter), composer Wolfgang Mozart (Jupiter), artist Paul Cezanne (Jupiter), playwright Eugene O'Neill (Uranus), astrologer Mohan Koparkar, political assassin Carlos the Jackal.

19 Libra

The iron fist. "Might makes right." Strong-willed and very determined to rise in the ranks. Usually a religious or a political side. This degree can indicate artistic talent.

Examples: U.S. President George Washington (Pluto), King Leopold II (Saturn), politician Georges Clemenceau (Mercury), dictator Adolf Hitler (Uranus), occultist Aleister Crowley, politician Margaret Thatcher, singer Lillie Langtry, comedian Lenny Bruce, actor Roger Moore, singer Paul Simon, U.S. Vice President Nelson Rockefeller (Ascendant), actress Sally Field (Ascendant), athlete John McEnroe (Ascendant), actor Jean-Claude Van Damme (Ascendant), entertainer Dick Gregory.

20 Libra

This is a softer degree in Libra. Sweet Alice. Very charming, they can nevertheless be outspoken. There is also a love of travel.

Examples: U.S. President Dwight Eisenhower, author Katherine Mansfield, political theorist Hannah Arendt, actor Yves Montand.

21 Libra

A powerful artistic area of Libra begins here. Literature is especially favored, probably because the Gemini decanate is coming in. The literary person. But all the arts are possible. Also political ambitions.

Examples: author C. P. Snow, poet e.e. cummings, author Guenter Grass, historian Arthur Schlesinger, philosopher Michel Foucault, author D.H. Lawrence (Moon), actress Lillian Gish.

22 Libra

Artistic power. There is great energy here and deep intelligence. The thinker. But they can be much too active for their own good.

Examples: artist Egon Schiele (Uranus), philosopher Nietzsche, playwright Oscar Wilde, playwright Arthur Miller, author D.H. Lawrence (Venus), author Thomas Mann (Jupiter), humorist P. G. Wodehouse, artist Edouard Manet (Moon), politician Henry Kissinger (Moon), businessman Lee Iacocca, actress Linda Darnell, actress Angela Lansbury.

23 Libra

Perhaps Libra's artistic genius reaches its height in this degree. Fixed star Arcturus, "star of the artists." Fixed star Spica. There is much love of beauty and science. A strong writer's degree.

Also a good actor's degree.

Examples: playwright Eugene O'Neill, author Emily Dickinson (Moon), author F. Scott Fitzgerald (Venus), author Jessica Mitford (Venus), poet Yeats (Saturn), politician Winston Churchill (Jupiter), actor Montgomery Clift, actress Rita Hayworth, politician David Ben-Gurion, dare-devil Evel Knievel, singer Laura Nyro.

24 Libra

Another actor's degree. Lover boy. But people with this degree are perhaps less talented, and experience relationship problems, possibly because of jealousy or a wandering eye.

Examples: actor George C. Scott, musician Chuck Berry, actor Jean-Claude Van Damme, author Michael Crichton (Venus and Mars), politician Pierre Trudeau, murderer Lee Harvey Oswald, author Simon Vestdijk.

25 Libra

This degree can indicate a writer. There is something more civilized, cultured, or poetical about them. The sophisticate.

Examples: author Miguel de Cervantes, author T.S. Eliot (Ascendant), politician John Profumo, singer Danii Minogue.

26 Libra

A sensitive, refined, and artistic degree. Can indicate a poet. On the other hand, these people can be rather naive and lack understanding at times. The poet.

Examples: composer Sergei Prokofiev (Moon), author T.S. Eliot (Mercury), artist Chagall (Jupiter), musician Freddie Mercury (Jupiter), singer Madonna (Jupiter), poet Arthur Rimbaud, philosopher John Dewey, dictator Adolf Hitler (Ascendant), athlete Mickey Mantle, author Art Buchwald.

27 Libra

This degree is stronger and steadier than most Libra degrees. Maybe the influence of Scorpio is coming in. Generally they have a gentle temper and a soothing influence. The compromiser. There is also intelligence.

Examples: composer Franz Liszt, scientist Alfred Nobel, playwright George Bernard Shaw (Mars), actor Bella Lugosi, actress Joan Fontaine.

28 Libra

Possibly the laziest degree in the zodiac. And not particularly lucky. Nevertheless, they frequently possess a truly philosophical spirit. A taste for literature, either as a reader or writer. A polite, civilized, and sophisticated degree. Very Libra. And also interested in their hair. The lazybones.

Examples: military leader Albrecht von Wallenstein (Mars), poet Rupert Brooke (Jupiter), actress Grace Kelly (Venus), poet Samuel Coleridge, actor Cary Grant (Ascendant), singer Frank Sinatra (Ascendant), artist Robert Raushenburg, activist Timothy Leary, actress Catherine Deneuve, actor Derek Jacobi, singer Dory Previn, dancer Ted Shawn, actress Carrie Fisher.

29 Libra

These people are usually artistic but they need a harmonious atmosphere surrounding them. There is much interest in meditation and the occult. "To know harmony is called the constant."—Lao Tzu.

Examples: entertainer Johnny Carson, activist Bobby Seale, poet Friedrich Schiller (Venus), Lord Alfred Douglas, spiritual master Meher Baba (Saturn), actor Ryan Reynolds.

Scorpio

0 Scorpio

Scorpio comes in with a great deal of strength—strength of character and of intelligence. But these people are also good-natured. Plus the usual big ego. But people with this degree can have a lot of trouble with partners; "It's my way or the highway."

Examples: actress Sarah Bernhardt, author Michael Crichton, dictator Rafael Trujillo, actor Kevin Kline.

1 Scorpio

The green-eyed monster. A strong music degree. Also a scientific side. A strong leader. Some of these people have problems with partners or lose them. A jealous degree.

Examples: composer Georges Bizet, composer Maurice Ravel (Jupiter), singer Helen Reddy, scientist Anton van Leeuwenhoek, astrologer R. C. Jansky, King James II, settler William Penn (Sun and Ascendant), Shah of Iran M. R. Pahlavi, murderer Klaus Barbie.

2 Scorpio

Strength of mind and character. Good degree for a politician. The statesman. There is also a concern for the mystical and the occult in early Scorpio degrees. And the traveller.

Examples: artist Pablo Picasso, explorer Richard E. Byrd, politician Francois Mitterand, politician Hillary Clinton, actor John Cleese, singer Katy Perry.

3 Scorpio

This degree reveals all the true qualities of Scorpio. Willpower, the mysterious reserve, and a penetrating mind. Writers. Meditation. The pacifist.

Examples: poet Dylan Thomas, politician Mohandas Gandhi (Mercury), philosopher John Dewey (Mercury), astrologer Marc Edmond Jones (Mercury), politician H. R. Haldeman.

4 Scorpio

This is a gentle degree of Scorpio and is associated with the poet. They are always in control. "Walk softly and carry a big stick."

Examples: author Sylvia Plath, actor Bruce Lee (Mars), scientist Jonas Salk, U.S. President Teddy Roosevelt, author Evelyn Waugh, murderer Perry Smith, actress Julia Roberts, actress Grace Kelly (Ascendant).

5 Scorpio

This is a macho, materialistic degree (Scorpio is a money sign). There is selfishness here, and they generally acquire what they go after. They can also be aggressive. A degree of healing. The materialist.

Examples: politician Franz von Papen, singer Fanny Brice, entrepreneur Bill Gates, actor Richard Dreyfuss, actress Winona Ryder, Prince Aly Khan (Jupiter), astrologer Nicholas Culpeper.

6 Scorpio

A medical degree. Hard worker. A very gentle degree. Some of these people are good poets.

Examples: poet Pierre de Ronsard (Venus), poet Paul Valery, politician Joseph Goebbels, singer Grace Slick. "A thing of beauty is a joy forever."—John Keats.

7 Scorpio

Hercules. Can indicate great physical strength and a beautiful physique. They are rather hard to fathom. Some are executives. A strong Ascendant degree.

Examples: athlete Charles Atlas, actor Bud Spencer, athlete Gentleman Jim Corbett (Saturn), athlete Babe Ruth (Saturn), possibly Christopher Columbus, architect Christopher Wren (Sun and Neptune), poet Ezra Pound, politician Chiang Kai-shek, actress Melina Mercouri, journalist Dan Rather, missionary David Livingstone (Ascendant), psychiatrist Sigmund Freud (Ascendant), philosopher Bertrand Russell (Ascendant), Manuel Garcia (Ascendant), comedian Red Skelton (Ascendant), actress Katherine Hepburn (Ascendant).

8 Scorpio

Strength and authority. An executive. This degree has many of the emotional challenges typical of Scorpio, including jealousy and possessiveness. They have blind spots. Nevertheless, they are passionate and have good minds.

Examples: artist Johannes Vermeer, author Stephen T. Crane, occultist Cheiro, publisher Larry Flynt.

9 Scorpio

These people are a mystery. Moreover, they are not always dependable. Some are orphans. The orphan.

Examples: actor Charlie Chaplin (Moon), activist Malcolm X (Saturn), media mogul Oprah Winfrey (Saturn), actor Burt Lancaster, actress Stefanie Powers.

10 Scorpio

These people like to play their little games. They're secretive or deceptive. The trickster. And sometimes they just like to play the clown.

Examples: Businessman P. T. Barnum (Uranus), entertainer Groucho Marx (Ascendant), entertainer Johnny Carson (Mercury), actor Peter Sellers (Saturn), Queen Marie Antoinette, U.S. President James Polk, U.S. President Warren G. Harding, author Andre Malraux, actor Charles Bronson.

11 Scorpio

This is a powerful degree. The strongman. A lot of the suspiciousness and jealousy of Scorpio is evidenced here.

Examples: religious leader Billy Sunday (Mars and Jupiter), actor Bruce Lee (Moon), actor Art Carney, comedian Roseanne Barr, businessman Alfred Heineken, photographer Robert Mapplethorpe, commentator Walter Cronkite.

12 Scorpio

One of the most beautiful degrees of Scorpio. Sympathy and understanding. Passionate and artistic. In addition, they can excel at business. A very sensual degree. Possibly a poet. Yet also stable and practical. Magnetic healing. The cowboy.

Examples: author Will Rogers, actor Roy Rogers, actress Vivien Leigh, astrologer Bil Tierney, musician Herman Brood.

13 Scorpio

A good business degree. The self-made man or woman. Both good and bad qualities. They have strong personalities and are stubborn. Can also be arrogant, isolated, and sometimes sneaky. They are often on the stage.

Examples: playwright Henry Ibsen (Jupiter), U.S. President Jimmy Carter (Moon), theologian Desiderius Erasmus, military leader T.E. Lawrence (Mars), actress Elke Sommer, actress Sally Field, composer Pyotr Tchaikovsky (Jupiter), U.S. President Ronald Reagan (Jupiter), actor Paul Newman, author Yukio Mishima (Saturn), politician Margaret Thatcher (Saturn), politician Condoleezza Rice (Saturn), author Sylvia Porter (Ascendant), musician Art Garfunkel, murderer Marc Dutroux.

14 Scorpio

Some identify this degree as weak, but this is not always the case. It is a business degree. These people are often complicated and difficult to understand. Still, they can be enthusiastic. A riddle.

Examples: composer John Philip Sousa, evangelist Billy Graham, scientist Madame Curie, singer Joan Sutherland, actor Alain Delon, author Albert Camus, singer Joni Mitchell.

15 Scorpio

Sometimes strong, sometimes weak. A business area. There seems to be some heavy or fatalistic influence at work here. None of the usual Scorpio persistence. An anomaly.

Examples: explorer James Cook, revolutionary Leon Trotsky, physician Christiaan Barnard, singer Patti Page, astrologer Marc Penfield, singer Rickie Lee Jones.

16 Scorpio

Painting or another artistic talent. Perhaps there is something kind here but they do get their problems with people. Astrology or astronomy. The star-gazer.

Examples: author Ivan Turgenev (Sun and Mercury), artist Edvard Munch (Jupiter), King Edward VII, actress Hedy Lamarr, U.S. Vice President Spiro Agnew, Sir Edmond Halley, astornomer C. E. Sagan, astrologer Charubel, astrologer Jeff Green (Ascendant).

17 Scorpio

A rather weak degree. There seems to be a lot of resentment associated with it; in addition, it is linked with intestinal health problems. Perhaps these natives must learn to become more cheerful, to be more optimistic. A certain sex appeal. Sour grapes.

Examples: photographer Linda McCartney (Moon), composer Dmitri Shostakovitch (Venus), actor Rock Hudson (Saturn), actor Richard Burton (Sun and Saturn), poet Friedrich von Schiller.

18 Scorpio

A ballerina. Sometimes a dancer. A writer. Nevertheless, this can be a degree of a great deal of Scorpio jealousy and distrust.

Examples: author Dostoyevsky, author Mark Twain (Mercury), poet Rimbaud (Mercury), poet Rainier Rilke (Jupiter), composer Ennio Morricone, author Kurt Vonnegut, actor Leonardo DiCaprio.

19 Scorpio

Perhaps the most powerful of all Scorpio degrees, for good or for evil. The cursed one. A lot of ambition and a great deal of success. They are strong and determined and certainly to be reckoned with. Often they end up happy as well. Fixed star North Scale.

Examples: revolutionary Sun Yat-sen, military leader George Patton, murderer Charles Manson, bank robber Billy the Kid (Moon), actress Grace Kelly, musician Neil Young, comedian Jonathan Winters, actress Demi Moore, actor Charlton Heston (Jupiter).

20 Scorpio

Macho. Another powerful degree. They do not back down from a challenge. Courage. A strong sex drive. Also interest in the occult.

Examples: actor Chris Noth, sculptor Benvenuto Cellini, sculptor Rodin, author Robert Louis Stevenson, King Hussein, actress Whoopi Goldberg.

21 Scorpio

This is a restless impulsive degree but also gives a love of home and children. A rather frustrating combination. The scatterbrain. Prone to wander.

Examples: composer Leopold Mozart, explorer Daniel Boone, Duchess of Windsor Wallis Simpson (Uranus), military leader Claus von Stauffenberg. author Sylvia Plath (Mercury), politician Condoleezza Rice.

22 Scorpio

This is the luckiest degree in Scorpio for money. The heiress. There is artistic talent. Nevertheless, there is something restless and scattered here. This degree may also produce leaders.

Examples: heiress Barbara Hutton, First Lady Mamie Eisenhower, Prince Charles, mililtary leader Count Zeppelin (Saturn), singer Diana Ross (Ascendant), artist Claude Monet, pianist Daniel Barenboim, actor Ed Asner, actor Sam Waterston, Emperor Tiberius, politician Jawaharlal Nehru, military leader Erwin Rommel, politician Joseph McCarthy.

23 Scorpio

People with this degree are anxious to acquire wealth, and almost as fortunate as the previous degree. But they usually have to work hard for their money. The "Horatio Alger" type. There is some refinement here.

Examples: murderer Bruno Hauptmann (Jupiter), author Stephen King (Jupiter), media mogul Oprah Winfrey (Mars), actress Julia Roberts (Neptune).

24 Scorpio

Also a strong desire for money. There is a variety of ability here. However, there is something gloomy and pessimistic here as well. Lingering sorrow.

Examples: composer Paul Hindemith, actor Rock Hudson, athlete Bob Mathias, actor Kurt Cobain (Neptune), actress Anna Nicole Smith (Neptune), director Martin Scorsese (Sun and Venus), singer Gordon Lightfoot.

25 Scorpio

There is a strong desire for money, and some of these people are even willing to risk their lives and break the law to acquire it. At all costs. Reckless, but not stupid.

Examples: actress Linda Evans, actor Danny DeVito.

26 Scorpio

The real strength of Scorpio returns. They are more compassionate. A moralist. An interest in the arts and philosophy. A good businessperson.

Examples: composer Carl Maria von Weber, U.S. President James Garfield, evangelist Billy Sunday, commentator Larry King, conductor Eugene Ormandy, politician Indira Gandhi, singer Kim Wilde, actress Jodie Foster, businessman Ferdinand de Lesseps, businessman Jack Welch, media mogul Ted Turner.

27 Scorpio

One of the best degrees in Scorpio. Nobility. The person of conscience. This is a strong degree for literature. They are honest, possess a good conscience, and have a positive moral influence over other people. "Here I stand, I can do no other. So help me God."—Martin Luther.

Examples: Theologian Martin Luther, poet Alfred Lord Tennyson (Saturn), sculptor Rodin (Jupiter), military leader T. E. Lawrence (Jupiter), playwright Noel Coward (Jupiter), activist Jesse Jackson (Venus), athlete Roy Campanella, actress Meg Ryan, commentator Dick Cavett, politician Joseph Biden, scientist Paracelsus.

28 Scorpio

Another good degree and they have many talents. They are confident. Yet there seems to be something strangely predestined or karmic here. Actors. The line of fate.

Examples: conductor Arturo Toscanini (Moon), musician Chrissie Hynde (Moon), politician Robert Kennedy, musician Peter Townsend, activist Timothy Leary (Venus), athlete Tiger Woods (Venus), photographer Robert Maplethorpe (Mars), astrologer Liz Greene (Ascendant), actress Gene Tierney, actress Bo Derek, actress Goldie Hawn, athlete Stan Musial, singer Bjork.

29 Scorpio

Another strong acting degree. Also many writers. There is a great deal of energy here and sometimes leadership. An academic influence. The college professor. Fixed star Bungula.

Examples: actress Jamie Lee Curtis, actor Matt Damon (Neptune), author Voltaire, author George Eliot, author Oliver Goldsmith, author Andre Gide, politician Charles de Gaulle, athlete Billie Jean King, artist Rene Magritte, composer Benjamin Britten, philosopher Nietzsche (Ascendant), author Thomas Wolfe (Ascendant), scientist Madame Curie (Mars), psychiatrist Carl Jung (Midheaven), astronomer Edwin Hubble, occultist Franz Hartmann.

Sagittarius

0 Sagittarius

Big egos. They love to travel. The adventurer. They are curious and in search of knowledge. People with this degree can be creative. It can indicate an outlaw. A degree of precision.

Examples: actress Scarlett Johansson, bank robber Billy the Kid.

1 Sagittarius

People with this degree strive for perfection. They also may become criminals. The bandit. There is something rebellious here. Both practical and creative. They remain optimistic. Great travelers.

Examples: gangster Lucky Luciano (Mars), composer Manuel De Falla, actor Franco Nero, theologian Junipera Serra, comedian Harpo Marx, Czar Peter I (Moon).

2 Sagittarius

The excitement seeker. These people really crave excitement and will do almost anything to get it. They're out to get their kicks! The party animal again. Crime is still possible here. Art or business.

Examples: gangster Lucky Luciano, murderer Ted Bundy, murderer Carlos the Jackal (Venus), comedian Lenny Bruce (Venus), dare-devil Evel Knievel (Venus), murderer Marc Dutroux

(Saturn), artist Toulouse-Lautrec, industrialist Andrew Carnegie, philosopher Baruch Spinoza, politician William F. Buckley, military leader Augusto Pinochet.

3 Sagittarius

This is a sweet degree, and like Cancer, is home-oriented. Some artistic talent, particularly painting or engraving. Home sweet home.

Examples: artist Agnolo Bronzino, cartoonist Charles Schulz, actor Robert Goulet, actress Christina Applegate.

4 Sagittarius

Artists. Musicians. Sharpness and keenness. They always do their best. There is real moral fiber here but they can become quite indignant when they feel the occasion calls for it. A straight-shooter. Typical Sagittarian optimism and confidence.

Examples: musician Jimi Hendrix, singer Tina Turner, media mogul Oprah Winfrey (Moon), murderer Bruno Hauptmann.

5 Sagittarius

This degree can indicate a depressed mentality and is very unlike Sagittarius in general. The victim of depression. However they sympathize with the downtrodden. Also a writing area, and verbal skills are strong here.

Examples: author Stefan Zweig, dancer Vaslav Nijinsky (Moon), playwright Eugene O'Neill (Jupiter), cartoonist Charles Addams (Jupiter), actress Vivien Leigh (Mercury), actress Anna Nicole Smith, actor Bruce Lee, military leader Ernst Roehm, actress Gloria Grahame, actor Ed Harris.

6 Sagittarius

A strong writing degree. Good mental abilities. Love of reading. In addition, some of these people suffer from feelings of claustrophobia. An intellectual.

Examples: astrologer Bruno Huber, author William Blake, author Friedrich Engels, author Shakespeare (Uranus), author Gogol (Neptune), author Edgar Allan Poe (Neptune), author Spinoza (Mercury), author Jane Austen (Mercury), author Dostoevsky (Mercury), author Albert Camus (Mercury), author Hans Christian Andersen (Jupiter), author Nancy Mitford, singer-songwriter Randy Newman.

7 Sagittarius

A strong interest in money. The plutocrat. This degree is also literary. They love the nice things of life, and often want to be left alone.

Examples: author Mark Twain, author Louisa May Alcott, politician Winston Churchill, producer Dick Clark, musician Chuck Mangione, poliltician Jacques Chirac.

8 Sagittarius

This is perhaps the most positive and optimistic degree of Sagittarius. Nothing seems to get them down. The eternal optimist. Remember, this is still the first decanate of Sagittarius.

Examples: King Charles I, actress Mary Martin, actor Richard Crenna, actor Ben Stiller, artist Pablo Picasso (Moon).

9 Sagittarius

This degree seems to have premonitions of the future. The clairvoyant. They are very energetic and very stubborn. Fatalistic. Also artistic. Fixed star Antares. Lots of lively and fiery activity. The diva.

Examples: occultist Paracelsus (Moon), philosopher Friedrich Nietzsche (Moon), singer Bob Geldof (Moon), author Kahlil Gibran (Venus), psychologist Timothy Leary (Ascendant), psychic Uri Geller (Mercury), astrologer Jeff Green, artist Georges Seurat, theologian John Calvin (Jupiter), singer Maria Callas (Sun and Ascendant), singer Bette Midler, artist Otto Dix, actor

Woody Allen, actress Julie Harris, comedian Richard Pryor, drug-lord Pablo Escobar, fashion designer Gianni Versace.

10 Sagittarius

This is a weak degree in general, but these people don't lack courage. Architects. They are good at organizing people. The group man or woman.

Examples: Akbar the Great, architect Christopher Wren (Mars), military leader George McClellan, singer Britney Spears, murderer Charles "Tex" Watson.

11 Sagittarius

These people are brave but very diplomatic. They are social. Sometimes fond of physical exercise. The sportsman. This degree can make a writer or an artist. Architects.

Examples: actor Brad Pitt (Ascendant), author Joseph Conrad, poet Rainer Maria Rilke, child psychologist Anna Freud, actress Daryl Hannah, actor Ozzy Osbourne, actress Julianne Moore.

12 Sagittarius

Writers. They have great energy. But they are fearful for their health. The hypochondriac.

Examples: author Thomas Carlyle, poet Christina Rossetti, dictator Francisco Franco, businessman Walt Disney, military leader George Custer, actor Jeff Bridges, actress Tyra Banks, singer Elvis Presley(Ascendant).

13 Sagittarius

These people are future-directed. Ahead of their time. It can make a good astrologer. They are in general non-conformist types but not without intelligence. A long journey.

Examples: philosopher Karl Marx (Midheaven), astrologer Robert Hand, astrologer Dane Rudhyar (Ascendant), businessman

George Westinghouse (Ascendant), actress Lillian Russell, murderer Richard Speck, singer Little Richard.

14 Sagittarius

This degree is very curious and always in search of knowledge. The eternal student. There are strong mental abilities and possibly literary talent. Sometimes an interest in the occult.

Examples: author Honore Balzac (Moon), author Charles Dickens (Moon), mathematician Albert Einstein (Moon), missionary Albert Schweitzer (Venus), anthropologist Margaret Mead (Mercury), astrologer Marc Edmond Jones (Mars), author Truman Capote (Jupiter), musician Dave Brubeck.

15 Sagittarius

People with this degree have good intuition, and are good teachers. Chances come early in life. Music. The early bloomer.

Examples: actress Ellen Burstyn, philosopher Noam Chomsky, musician Gregg Allman, singer Tom Waits, musician Jim Morrison, musician Buddy Holly (Jupiter), actress Brigitte Bardot (Ascendant), composer Sibelius

16 Sagittarius

These people like to enjoy themselves. Good-time Charlie. But they should be especially cautious of smoking. There is some artistic talent here.

Examples: Sculptress Camille Claudel, sculptor Aristide Maillol, actor Lee J. Cobb, singer Sammy Davis Jr., actor David Carradine, singer Elizabeth Schwarzkopf, actress Kim Basinger, politician Tip O'Neill, entertainer Flip Wilson.

17 Sagittarius

Artistic ability continues in this degree, especially for music. They have a fiery artistic temperament, but are rather innocent and childish underneath. The man of feeling. Bad for smoking.

Examples: Composer Wolfgang Mozart (Moon and Pluto), composer Hector Berlioz (Mars), singer Pavarotti (Mars), composer Ennio Morricone (Saturn), Sir Philip Sidney, inventor Eli Whitney, author Emily Dickinson, aritst Renoir (Jupiter), mathematician Augusta Ada Byron, actor Douglas Fairbanks (Moon), artist Diego Rivera, actor Kirk Douglas, actor John Malkovich, actress Teri Hatcher.

18 Sagittarius

This is another degree that indicates potential for lung problems; these people, especially, should not smoke. Asthma. They are often successful in business, and many artists have planets here as well. Zeal and passion. Writers. The man of sensibility.

Examples: Author Jonathan Swift, composer Hector Berlioz, author Aleksandr Solzhenitsyn, spiritual leader Bhagwan Rajneesh, actor Kenneth Branagh.

19 Sagittarius

The man about town. There is lots of ardor and fire in people with this degree. The real enthusiasm of Sagittarius reaches a high point here. They have strong personalities and passionate feelings; plus, a clever and subtle mind. And they come into contact with important people and celebrities, rub elbows with the rich and famous. Music and writing. Danger from fire. Especially bad for smoking.

Examples: occultist Cheiro (Ascendant), author Robert Burns (Moon), businessman Howard Hughes (Moon), heiress Christina Onassis, author Gustave Flaubert, producer Carlo Ponti, singer Frank Sinatra, singer Brenda Lee, singer Madonna (Saturn).

20 Sagittarius

La dolce vita. This is a weak degree, but these people are polite and clever. Good with groups. Medical area. A pleasing personality.

Examples: actor Edward G. Robinson, poet Kenneth Patchen, singer Connie Francis, singer Dionne Warwick.

21 Sagittarius

This degree seems to bring out feelings of paranoia in many people. They have many doubts and fears to deal with. But there is intelligence here. The paranoiac.

Example: poet Ezra Pound (Venus).

22 Sagittarius

People witht this degree fight for justice and for the underdog. The freedom fighter. A good attorney. Some are revolutionaries. Some can be violent.

Examples: Politician Maximilien de Robespierre (Pluto), philosopher Friedrich Engels (Mercury), author Henrik Ibsen (Mars), author Henry David Thoreau (Neptune), politician Winston Churchill (Venus), journalist Drew Pearson, singer Bob Geldof (Ascendant), actress Patty Duke, Emperor Nero.

23 Sagittarius

These people seem to have their fair share of emotional problems. There is a jealous side. But there is another side which can be brave and honest. A pure conscience.

Examples: author Noel Coward, politician Margaret Chase Smith, anthropologist Margaret Mead, actress Liv Ullmann, actor Don Johnson.

24 Sagittarius

A degree of genius, but often gloomy and pessimistic which is precisely the opposite of what we expect from Sagittarius. The tragic artist or lonely genius. Nonetheless, there is a great deal of poetic imagination residing here.

Examples: composer Beethoven, artist Wassily Kandinsky,

compsoer Brahms (Moon), actor Montgomery Clift (Moon), author Rudhyard Kipling (Mercury and Mars), author William Wordsworth (Jupiter), artist Vincent Van Gogh (Jupiter), industrialist John Paul Getty, playwright Eugene O'Neill (Mars), cartoonist Charles Addams (Mercury), First Lady Jacqueline Kennedy (Saturn), singer Janis Joplin (Mars), actor Anthony Hopkins (Moon), author Jane Austen, poet J. G.Whittier, philosopher George Santayana, artist Michelangelo (Ascendant).

25 Sagittarius

Artistic power, but overall this is a weaker degree. These people have dreams of grandeur. Something very stubborn and rebellious here, if not altogether tyrannical. The anarchist.

Examples: Archduke Franz Ferdinand, poet Robert Burns (Pluto), politician Willy Brandt, conductor Arthur Fiedler, musician Keith Richards, actor Brad Pitt, author Andre Gide (Mars), actress Sharon Stone (Saturn), musician Randy Newman (Moon), actor Charlie Sheen (Moon), actress Milla Jovovich.

26 Sagittarius

A degree of genius. The child prodigy. Literature is strongly favored. Can be a leader. Much all-round ability.

Examples: artist Paul Klee, producer Steven Spielberg, author Graham Greene (Uranus), politician Leonid Brezhnev, revolutionary Joseph Stalin, Mary Queen of Scots, composer Anton Dvorak (Saturn), athlete Ty Cobb, actress Betty Grable, author Michel de Montaigne (Jupiter), revolutionary Karl Marx (Neptune), singer Christina Aguilera, actress Katie Holmes, singer Edith Piaf, actor Ray Liotta.

27 Sagittarius

This is a weaker degree. Others are often jealous or envious of their efforts, which can produce conflict. There can be writing talent here. Thou shalt not covet thy neighbor's ass."—The Holy Bible

Examples: U.S. President Warren G. Harding (Jupiter), John Milton, author Herman Hesse (Jupiter), author Jean Genet, psychic Uri Geller.

28 Sagittarius

This degree is steady and sensible in tone. There is real strength here. This degree might make a good lawyer or a writer. A head on his shoulders.

Examples: politician Kurt Waldheim, author Heinrich Boll, actor Jake Gyllenhaal.

29 Sagittariuis

The headman. People with this degree want to be the boss. But strangely there is something childish and unsure about them. Nevertheless they often make good entertainers or actors. They also like to stay in good physical condition.

Examples: politician Disraeli, fashion designer Louis Vuitton (Uranus), dictator Joseph Stalin (Venus), murderer Heinrich Himmler (Saturn), U.S. President Richard Nixon (Mars), composer Giacomo Puccini, actress Jane Fonda, musician Frank Zappa, actor Kiefer Sutherland, media mogul Oprah Winfrey (Ascendant).

Capricorn

0 Capricorn

Strong egos. This is a very conservative degree that has most of the Capricorn traits: patient, ambitious, and hard-working. A little bit bourgeois. The model citizen.

Example: Lady Bird Johnson.

1 Capricorn

The merry widow. These people are serious types, although they also have a sense of humor. They are confident and handle people well.

Examples: seer Nostradamus, politician Helmut Schmidt, actress Carla Bruni.

2 Capricorn

The self-confidence continues. There is also a high degree of intelligence here. A good business degree. The tycoon. Sometimes an interest in the stars.

Examples: businessman Howard Hughes, media mogul Rupert Murdoch (Ascendant), politician Anwar Sadat, astronomer Tycho Brahe, Cosima Liszt (wife of the German composer), actress Ava Gardner, singer Ricky Martin.

3 Capricorn

This degree is powerful and these people can do almost anything they desire. The physical constitution is very strong, and often the life expectancy is longer than average. They are ambitious, show good judgment, and strive for perfection. A hotel owner.

Examples: author Johann Goethe (Mars), businessman Conrad Hilton, American Red Cross founder Clara Barton (Sun and Uranus), actor Rod Serling, author Carlos Casteneda, business-woman Helena Rubinstein, actress Sissy Spacek, singer Annie Lennox.

4 Capricorn

The big brother. A powerful degree. They have strong will-power. There can be an interest in science or the arts. They are usually warm and hospitable.

Examples: politician Mao, author Henry Miller, actor Richard Widmark, scientist Louis Pasteur (Sun and Neptune), astrono-mer J. E. Bode (Mercury), scientist Charles Richter (Saturn), ac-tor Spencer Tracy (Saturn), presidential secretary Rose Mary Woods, entertainer Steve Allen.

5 Capricorn

This degree can also indicate a scientist. They are hard workers, practical and down-to-earth. Also a basic warm friendliness, but perhaps they are too trusting. A scientific discovery.

Examples: scientist Louis Pasteur (Venus), physician William Masters, actress Marlene Dietrich, anarchist Auguste Vaillant, actor Gerard Depardieu, actor Denzel Washington.

6 Capricorn

This degree is weak. They are very shy and withdrawn. Jealousy seems to come in here. They have their problems with relation-ships. Sometimes artistic. The introvert.

Example: composer Dmitri Shostakovitch (Moon).

7 Capricorn

The president or prime minister. Jealousy. Sometimes this degree indicates a politician. They are not always fortunate.

Examples: Sir William Cecil (Pluto), U.S. President James Monroe (Moon), politician Gladstone, U.S. President Andrew Johnson, U.S. President Woodrow Wilson, Madame de Pompadour, politician Jawaharlal Nehru (Jupiter), actress Mary Tyler Moore, actor Jon Voight, actor Ted Danson, actor Jude Law.

8 Capricorn

This degree indicates creative power. There is often the restless and sensitive nature of the artist. There is true nobility here. A lofty vision. Material wealth interests them little, but they are ambitious.

Examples: artist Peter Paul Rubens (Saturn), poet A. E. Housman (Moon), poet Robert Burns (Jupiter), actor Charlie Chaplin (Jupiter), fashion designer Don Loper (Uranus), fashion designer Diane Von Furstenberg, politician Al E. Smith, musician Pablo Casals, athlete Sandy Koufax, actor Russ Tamblyn, athlete Tiger Woods, singer Patti Smith.

9 Capricorn

A less important degree. Yet these people are discrete and confident. Perhaps some artistic influence. They need patience as they will be tested. "Adversity's sweet milk, philosophy, to comfort thee."—Romeo and Juliet.

Examples: Author Rudyard Kipling, businesswoman Elizabeth Arden, Nazi hunter Simon Wiesenthal, singer John Denver, actor Anthony Hopkins, actor Val Kilmer, astrologer Doris Hebel.

10 Capricorn

An artist's degree. These people seem to yearn for a position of authority and very often they are successful. The director.

Examples: artist Matisse, author J. D. Salinger, philosopher

Cicero, author Rudyard Kipling (Jupiter), military leader George Marshall, FBI Director J. Edgar Hoover, politiican Edward Kennedy (Ascendant), choreographer Maurice Bejart, director Gus Trikonis, singer Donna Summer, astrologer Noel Tyl.

11 Capricorn

The dictator. These people are very secretive and highly ambitious for power. They have an incredible memory. The occult.

Examples: King Louis XVI (Saturn), dictator Joseph Stalin (Mercury), murderer Klaus Barbie (Jupiter), Senator Barry Goldwater, philosopher Niccolo Machiavelli (Ascendant), author E. M. Forster, occultist Charubel (Neptune), psychic Edgar Cayce (Mars).

12 Capricorn

Too clever by half. Too smart for your own good. This is a weaker degree. But these people are clever, and enjoy their little games. An ability for business begins in this degree of Capricorn.

Examples: author J. R. R. Tolkien, musician Stephen Stills, director Sergio Leone, actor Mel Gibson.

13 Capricorn

Macho. This is one of the strongest and most aggressive degrees in Capricorn. They act superior but they are also honorable. They have a sense of adventure. This is also a business degree.

Examples: athlete Floyd Patterson, U.S. President Dwight D. Eisenhower (Mars), entertainer Johnny Carson (Moon), murderer Lee Harvey Oswald (Moon), scientist Sir Isaac Newton, inventor Louis Braille, actress Marion Davies, actress Jane Wyman, actor Paul Newman (Mercury and Ascendant), actress Dyan Cannon.

14 Capricorn

One of the strongest artistic degrees in Capricorn, especially for fine artists and graphic artists. The draughtsman. Fixed star Vega. Could be a writer. Business area. Also mathematics.

Examples: artist Gustave Paul Dore, businessman Walt Disney (Saturn), author John Milton (Mercury), author Jacob Grimm, author Alan Watts, author Umberto Eco, politician Konrad Adenauer, actress Diane Keaton, actor Robert Duvall (Sun and Saturn).

15 Capricorn

A backslapper. A soft degree. These people are too preoccupied with gaining the approval of others. Not very typical of Capricorn. Some significance in music.

Examples: composer Alexander Scriabin, astronomer Johannes Kepler, poet Carl Sandburg, businessman John DeLorean, mystic Yogananda.

16 Capricorn

This degree indicates a good student, and sometimes a thinker. There are many possibilities here for good or evil. Often successful. "For the rain it falleth on the good and the evil alike."—The Bible.

Examples: Psychologist William James (Mercury), Saint Bernadette, entertainer Komar, actress Loretta Young, cartoonist Charles Addams, actor Nicolas Cage.

17 Capricorn

Probably the most creative degree in Capricorn, especially for music. The singer. But all forms of art are possible. Frequently something sweet and gentle in the character, but this degree can also be connected to crime.

Examples: Singer Elvis Presley, singer Shirley Bassey, singer David Bowie, singer Perry Como (Jupiter), singer Tommy Sands (Jupiter), composer Ludwig von Beethoven (Pluto), composer Francois Poulenc, philosopher Simone de Beauvoir, poet John Dryden (Ascendant), author Jules Verne (Neptune), actor Lawrence Olivier (Mars), actor Marlon Brando (Mars), U.S. President Millard Fillmore.

18 Capricorn

This is an anti-social degree. The rebel without a cause. These people are sometimes dishonest and difficult to get along with.

Examples: Illustrator-author Aubrey Beardsley (Ascendant), musician James Dean (Saturn), artist Andy Warhol (Saturn), military leader Primo de Rivera, impresario Rudolph Bing, actress Gracie Fields, singer Crystal Gayle, medium Phyllis Givens.

19 Capricorn

A strong degree that is often associated with a forceful personality. Determination. Never say die. They are almost impossible to deter or defeat. Also a sense of integrity. "What does not kill you makes you stronger."—Nietzsche.

Examples: physician Andreas Vesalius, Lady Randolph Churchill, U.S. President Richard Nixon, singer Joan Baez, actor Sal Mineo, actress Linda Lovelace, singer Rod Stewart, military leader George Patton (Moon).

20 Capricorn

A weaker degree. Changeable disposition. Some vanity but no real confidence. Dancers. Limited horizons.

Examples: astrologer John Gadbury, actress Christina Aguilera (Mars), athlete George Foreman.

21 Capricorn

This degree can be associated with the excellent professor. They are capable of deep research. Science, philosophy, psychology, and religion are all possible options. The scholar.

Examples: military leader Robert E. Lee (Jupiter), psychologist William James, Swami Vivekananda, scientist Charles Darwin (Moon), physician Havelock Ellis (Mercury), philosopher Bertrand Russell (Saturn), military leader Joseph Joffre.

22 Capricorn

Another powerful personality. Often an artist. They have many interests, both for the old and the new. There is a spiritual side. But they can be very complicated people, at times kind and generous and at other times cold and critical. A real riddle. The sphinx.

Examples: politician Alexander Hamilton, military leader Hermann Goering, author Jack London, author Horatio Alger, actor Robert Stack, author Samuel Johnson (Ascendant), singer Bono (Ascendant), seer Nostradamus (Neptune), theosophist Madame Blavatsky (Neptune).

23 Capricorn

These people are very direct and blunt. The "tough customer." And their expectations tend to be too high. But underneath they are quite pleasant.

Examples: King Henry VIII (Uranus), author Thomas Paine (Moon), singer Nina Simone (Moon), politician Paul von Hindenburg (Ascendant), murderer Carlos the Jackal (Jupiter), author Jean Genet (Uranus), author Yukio Mishima, actress Gwen Verdon, singer L. L. Cool J, actor Orlando Bloom.

24 Capricorn

Honest as the day is long. These people are reliable and sincere. Music.

Examples: art critic John Ruskin (Mercury), theologian Albert

Schweitzer (Sun and Mercury), author John Steinbeck (Saturn), politician A. G. Nasser, actress Faye Dunaway.

25 Capricorn

This is likely the most conformist degree in Capricorn. These are the people who worry about what the neighbors will think. Deeply conservative and formal. The conformist.

Examples: author Henry James (Saturn), dictator Fulgencio Batista, activist Martin Luther King, actor Lloyd Bridges.

26 Capricorn

This is a very rebellious and anti-social degree. They are at odds with society. A lot of hostility and frustration seems to be located here. The nonconformist.

Examples: revolutionary Toussaint L'Ouverture (Uranus), actress Lucille Ball (Uranus), poet Ezra Pound (Ascendant), union leader James Hoffa (Mars), actor James Dean (Mercury), actor Jim Carrey, playwright Moliere, politician Lloyd George, physician Tom Dooley, actor Cary Grant, singer Francoise Hardy, actor James Earl Jones.

27 Capricorn

There is something rough and rugged in this degree. A man's man; a woman's woman. They are strong characters but fundamentally simple and straight-forward. A lot of grit and determination. Ambitious.

Examples: athlete Muhammad Ali, bullfighter Manuel Garcia, inventor Benjamin Franklin, U.S. President Abraham Lincoln (Moon), actor Richard Harris (Moon), politician Richard J. Daley (Saturn), athlete Rocky Marciano (Ascendant), entertainer Danny Kaye.

28 Capricorn

This degree produces a very responsible person. They make good leaders. They are logical thinkers and very ambitious. "Life is real! Life is earnest!"—H. W. Longfellow.

Examples: Captain John Smith, military leader Robert E. Lee, Emperor Napoleon (Moon), politician Indira Gandhi (Moon), politician Robert Kennedy (Moon), author Edgar Allan Poe (Sun and Mercury), author Somerset Maugham (Mercury and Venus), artist Cezanne, gangster Al Capone, poet A.A. Milne, actor Oliver Hardy, singer Janis Joplin, actor Kevin Costner, politician Daniel Webster.

29 Capricorn

There is a note of melancholy in this degree. It often indicates a poet or a scientist. There is a spiritual or meditative side to their nature. But always something heavy and ponderous. "Tears, idle tears, I know not what they mean."—Tennyson.

Examples: Director Frederico Fellini, composer Brahms (Neptune), author Jonathan Swift (Saturn), businessman Walt Disney (Venus), author Virginia Woolf (Venus), singer Elvis Presley (Venus), astronomer Johann Elert Bode, author Alexander Woolcott, actor Telly Savalas, actress Patricia Neal, singer Dolly Parton.

Aquarius

0 Aquarius

Aquarius comes in with a great deal of energy, and this degree can indicate a leader. There is curiosity, new ideas, and perhaps genius. The inventor, the visionary. Big ego.

Examples: military leader Stonewall Jackson, U.S. President and inventor Thomas Jefferson (Ascendant), poet W. B. Yeats (Ascendant), activist Ralph Nader (Ascendant), philosopher Nietzsche (Saturn), art critic John Ruskin (Jupiter), dancer Ruth St. Denis, fashion designer Christian Dior, athlete Jack Nicklaus, entertainer Benny Hill, actress Geena Davis, actor Steve Reeves.

1 Aquarius

Often misses the boat. Johnnie-come-lately. They are very intelligent and curious, but also quickly bored. Maybe their expectations are unrealistic.

Examples: Duke of Windsor (Ascendant), choreographer George Balanchine, singer Placido Domingo, actor John Hurt, singer Sam Cooke, actress Linda Blair.

2 Aquarius

This degree reveals true genius. The flash of insight. A powerful curiosity, chiefly intellectual. Could be a leader. Or a writer. There is danger of obesity. Science and philosophy are favored.

Examples: artist Manet, U.S. President Dwight D. Eisenhower (Jupiter), U.S. President Richard Nixon (Uranus), philosopher Machiavelli (Moon), Senator John McCain (Moon), Lord Byron, playwright August Strindberg, author Agatha Christie (Jupiter), seer Nostradamus (Venus). author Michel de Montaigne (Pluto), actress Jeanne Moreau, actress Ann Sothern, actor Rutger Hauer.

3 Aquarius

An artistic area. They have an odd or eccentric side. Some desire to play the martyr. Nevertheless, they are quite friendly. "A sea of troubles."—Shakespeare

Examples: author Marie-Henri Stendhal, musician John Lennon (Moon), artist Michelangelo (Jupiter), Frederick the Great, politician John Hancock, Princess Caroline, actress Natassja Kinski.

4 Aquarius

A flashy personality. They will not go unnoticed. The exhibitionist. Writing talent; serious mental abilities. However, emotionally they are rather impersonal.

Examples: singer Gypsy Rose Lee (Jupiter), theologian James Pike (Uranus), dare-devil Evel Knievel (Ascendant), murderer Charles Manson (Moon), actress Gennifer Flowers, author Edith Wharton, musician Neil Diamond, artist Robert Motherwell, actress Sharon Tate.

5 Aquarius

The most rebellious degree in Aquarius. In particular they love to shock people. A dangerous degree for traveling. A good writer's degree as well. The rebel. This degree illustrates Uranus' influence on the sign Aquarius.

Examples: activist Angela Davis, comedian John Belushi, director Roger Vadim, singer Eartha Kitt, musician Eddie Van Halen, Rousseau (Jupiter), U.S. President William McKinley (Jupiter),

Princess Diana (Jupiter), poet Robert Burns, author Somerset Maugham (Sun and Saturn), conductor Wilhelm Furtwangler, author Virginia Woolf.

6 Aquarius

This is the most conservative degree in Aquarius. Perfectionists. Musical talent. The arch-conservative. This degree illustrates the influence of the old ruler, Saturn, on the sign Aquarius.

Examples: philosopher Francis Bacon (Mercury), U.S. President George Washington (Mercury), military leader Douglas MacArthur, author Lewis Carroll, industrialist Henry Ford (Moon), U.S. President Franklin Delano Roosevelt (Venus), composer Gustave Holst (Ascendant), James Stewart (Ascendant), actor Paul Newman, cartoonist Jules Feiffer, composer Edouard Lalo, athlete Wayne Gretzky.

7 Aquarius

There is potential for musical genius in this degree. The composer. Perhaps they have a perfect pitch. But some of these natives are difficult to understand.

Examples: composer Mozart, composer Bizet (Neptune), philosopher Friedrich von Schelling, King Wilhelm II, Titanic captain E. J. Smith, artist Jackson Pollock, actress Donna Reed, comedian Roseanne Barr (Ascendant), actor Alan Alda.

8 Aquarius

This degree also creates unusual personalities. But they are thinkers and often writers, too. Also, they certainly have emotional problems in their relationships. A unique person.

Examples: military leader Charles George Gordon, author Anton Chekhov, author Romain Rolland, actor John Forsythe, author Germaine Greer, media mogul Oprah Winfrey, politician Nicolas Sarkozy.

9 Aquarius

Forceful but also diplomatic They can be a bit stiff and formal. This degree and the following two indicate people who are good at handling others. A real individual.

Examples: philosopher Francis Bacon (Ascendant), author Thomas Paine, U.S. President William McKinley, composer Frederick Delius, actor W. C. Fields, actor Victor Mature, actor Tom Selleck, author Colette.

10 Aquarius

These natives are proud and outspoken. But they waste a lot of their energy. There is also a conservative streak, some are leaders, and others are famous. Diplomacy. The mediator.

Examples: author Norman Mailer, actor Gene Hackman, Queen Beatrix, actress Vanessa Redgrave, U.S. Vice President Dick Cheney, politician Otto von Bismarck (Saturn), comedian Dick Martin.

11 Aquarius

This degree also produces fame and leadership. The VIP. However, people with this degree can be headstrong and violent.

Examples: U.S. President Franklin Delano Roosevelt, athlete Jackie Robinson (Sun and Moon), actress Tallulah Bankhead, singer Mario Lanza, actor Clark Gable, author Muriel Spark, astrologer C.E.O. Carter.

12 Aquarius

A superiority complex. The intellectual snob. Extremely artistic. A great love of beauty. Music especially favored. "There is no excellent beauty that hath not some strangeness in the proportion."—Lord Bacon.

Examples: Sir Francis Bacon, inventor Ben Franklin (Mercury), playwright Tennesse Williams (Moon), artist Rodin (Neptune), composer Franz Schubert, musician Stan Getz, singer Renata

Tebaldi, singer Graham Nash, psychiatrist Carl Jung (Ascendant), musician Jim Morrison (Ascendant), singer Lisa Marie Presley, singer Justin Timberlake, musician Neil Young (Moon), singer Britney Spears (Moon), athlete Muhammed Ali (Moon), actor Brandon Lee, Princess Stephanie of Monaco.

13 Aquarius

Hubris. This is a very proud and belligerent degree, but also very artistic. Particularly literature. There is often something upsetting or fateful in their lives. Yet they continue to remain flexible.

Examples: author James Joyce, author James Michener, author Ayn Rand, actress Farrah Fawcett, physician Havelock Ellis, astrologer Carroll Righter, rapist Frederick Coe.

14 Aquarius

Love of the beautiful. An artist's degree. But they are eccentric in their habits. They are often restless and have times when they need to let it out. "Let's rock and roll!"

Examples: singer Janis Joplin (Venus), composer Mendelssohn, author Lewis Carroll (Uranus), singer Billie Holiday (Uranus), author Gertrude Stein (Sun and Mercury), aviator Charles Lindbergh, composer Tchaikovsky (Neptune), author Emile Zola (Neptune), author Thomas Hardy (Neptune), composer Anton Dvorak (Neptune), artist Renoir (Ascendant).

15 Aquarius

Artistic power reaches its height in this degree of Aquarius. Music, literature, and all other forms of art are possible. Also they like to read and to sport. It contributes to good will towards everyone. The universal ambassador.

Examples: artist Leonardo da Vinci (Mars), composer Handel (Venus), philosopher Simone de Beauvoir (Venus), author Byron (Pluto), artist Renoir (Neptune), artist Fernand Leger, singer Alice Cooper, actress Ida Lupino, activist Betty Friedan.

16 Aquarius

The enthusiast. Great energy and often spirituality. They are real individuals. There are sudden changes in the life. Much inspiration.

Examples: poet Rainer Maria Rilke (Moon), comedian Rip Torn, actress Zsa Zsa Gabor, politician Adlai Stevenson, U.S. President Ronald Reagan, businessman Citroen.

17 Aquarius

These people may end up sick or isolated. A rather sad degree. The recluse. Sometimes they come across to others as being too proud.

Examples: author Charles Dickens, athlete Babe Ruth, pianist Claudio Arrau, actress Mamie Van Doren, actor Roman Novarro.

18 Aquarius

This is one of the most brilliant degrees in Aquarius. Especially for literature. The author. Often a medical degree. They may choose their own direction in life. However, some of these people become isolated.

Examples: author Jules Verne, art critic John Ruskin, author Johann Goethe (Uranus) scientist Alfred Nobel (Uranus), author Henry David Thoreau (Ascendant), author Robert Louis Stevenson (Ascendant), artist Paul Klee (Ascendant), Wallis Simpson (Ascendant), author Virginia Woolf (Mercury), author H. Rider Haggard (Moon), director Orson Welles (Moon), author John Steinbeck (Venus), physician Alfred Adler, astrologer Joan McEvers, actor James Dean, actor James Spader, actor Chris Rock, U.S. President Barack Obama (Ascendant).

19 Aquarius

A very successful, intelligent, and versatile degree. Most likely to succeed. Artistic. Actors. An aura of confidence.

Examples: military leader William Sherman, astrologer Evangeline Adams, author Sinclair Lewis, artist Franz Marc, burlesque entertainer Gypsy Rose Lee (Sun and Venus), actress Lana Turner, actor Jack Lemmon, actor Nick Nolte, author Jacqueline Susann (Ascendant), businesswoman Elle Macpherson (Saturn).

20 Aquarius

People with this degree move at a slower yet steadier pace, and they have a great deal of common sense. The slow-goer. A strong degree for women.

Examples: actress Mia Farrow, singer Leontine Price, singer Carole King, astrologer Marion March, actor Robert Wagner, actor Joe Pesci.

21 Aquarius

These people have a great deal of strength and willpower, but they can be quite critical of others. They are good at public relations. The publicist.

Examples: King Farouk, author Charles Lamb, poet Bertold Brecht, labor leader John L. Lewis (Mercury), activist Angela Davis (Moon), director Joseph Mankiewicz, actor Burt Reynolds, athlete Mark Spitz, singer Roberta Flack.

22 Aquarius

Great energy and strength. Original thinking. Can also be violent. Perhaps they are merely over-sexed. The libido.

Examples: psychologist Virginia Johnson, scientist Leo Spitz, labor leader John L. Lewis, entertainer Jimmy Durante, director Gian-Franco Zeffirelli, actor Leslie Nielsen, politician Sarah Palin.

23 Aquarius

The universal genius. And possibly this is the most brilliant degree in the zodiac. Physical vitality and a sense of humor. Good degree for physicians. They are usually idealistic and possess a sympathy for humanity. The best of Aquarius emerges here.

Examples: U.S. President Abraham Lincoln, scientist Charles Darwin, philosopher Karl Marx (Ascendant), author Jean Paul Sartre (Moon), U.S. President John Kennedy (Uranus), musician Yehudi Menuhin (Uranus), actor Lorne Greene, author Georges Simenon, Nell Gwyn (mistress to King Charles II), fashion designer Emmanuel Ungaro, actor Oliver Reed, actress Jennifer Aniston.

24 Aquarius

Madame Bovary. Strangely naive and tragic. But they are strong and never back down from a fight.

Examples: Lord Randolph Churchill, actress Kim Novak, author Jack London (Saturn), author George Segal, actress Meg Tilly, entertainer Jerry Springer, singer Robbie Williams.

25 Aquarius

The other "great lover" degree, or questionable morals. There can be frustration and an anti-social attitude. Or the pure rebel.

Examples: poet Byron (Venus), conductor Arturo Toscanini (Jupiter), actress Claudia Cardinale (Jupiter), entertainer Marcello Mastroianni (Mars), author Truman Capote (Mars), singer Elvis Presley (Saturn), Princess Diana (Moon), actor John Barrymore, actor Cesar Romero, entertainer Jack Benny, First Lady Bess Truman, politician Maximilien de Robespierre (Ascendant), singer Janis Joplin (Ascendant), author Thomas Paine (Jupiter), labor leader James Hoffa.

26 Aquarius

An astrology area begins in this degree and continues to the end of Aquarius. These people have lots of ideas but are not always perfectly logical. A labyrinth. Music. Often successful. Determination.

Example: King Louis XV.

27 Aquarius

This is a strong degree, and these people are intelligent and intellectual. Occult interests. There is good will and hospitality, but a violent temper as well. A hothead.

Examples: Sir Thomas More, scientist Sir Isaac Newton (Venus), scientist Francis Galton, Baron Rothchild (Moon), poet Dylan Thomas (Moon), mathematician A. N. Whitehead, mathematician Albert Einstein (Jupiter), athlete Max Baer, athlete John McEnroe, activist Huey Newton, singer Sonny Bono.

28 Aquarius

This is the gambler's degree. They will risk everything on a bet, including their lives. Russian roulette. There are also artistic and occult influences. Often a nonconformist.

Examples: bank robber Jesse James (Neptune), industrialist Howard Hughes (Mars and Saturn), author-editor Helen Gurley Brown, actor Matt Dillon (Sun and Mars), businseswoman Paris Hilton (Sun and Mercury), mystic Ramakrishna.

29 Aquarius

"Don't stand so close to me." A highly intelligent and creative degree. Music and acting are favored. But they get their fair share of personal problems; they must learn detachment.

Examples: artist Max Klinger, musician Juan Orozco, musician Yoko Ono, actor Lee Marvin, actor John Travolta, actress Cybill Shepherd, actress Molly Ringwald, politician John Warner.

Pisces

0 Pisces

Pisces begins with a high level of enlightenment. Big readers. Music is strong. These people are friendly, kind, but also preoccupied with themselves. A person of culture. "A cheerful intelligent face is the end of culture, and success enough."—R.W. Emerson.

Examples: author Anais Nin (Jupiter), conductor Karl Bohm (Ascendant), fashion designer Gloria Vanderbilt, director John Frankenheimer, activist Karen Silkwood, politician Gordon Brown.

1 Pisces

Music and poetry. They are capable of serious study in the arts or sciences. Financially fortunate. A congenial nature.

Examples: poet W. H. Auden, singer Mary Garden, singer Nancy Wilson, singer Kurt Cobain, singer Prince (Moon), artist Leonardo da Vinci (Jupiter), artist Rembrandt (Jupiter), director Robert Altman, heiress Patty Hearst, socialite Ivana Trump, athlete Bobby Unser, actor Sidney Poitier.

2 Pisces

A musical degree. There is an intellectual influence here. Yet there is also a contradictory element here as well—sometimes lazy, sometimes active and violent. The sea god Proteus.

Examples: composer Leo Delibes, singer Nina Simone, composer Handel (Neptune), theologian J. H. Newman, author Anais Nin, politician Ted Kennedy, director Sam Peckinpah, artist Michelangelo (Moon), artist Paul Klee (Moon), singer Elvis Presley (Moon), author Victor Hugo (Venus), author Gertrude Stein (Ascendant), artist Gauguin (Neptune).

3 Pisces

One of the most powerful degrees in Pisces. The Renaissance man or woman. Music. They are capable of great leadership. Literature is very strong here and they are capable of deep thinking. Generally good-natured. Lucky with finances. Fixed star Formalhaut.

Examples: composer Johan Sebastian Bach (Neptune), musician Stan Getz (Jupiter), U.S. President George Washington, philosopher Schopenhauer, artist Leonardo da Vinci (Moon), artist Seurat (Moon), poet Edna St. Vincent Millay, poet Boris Pasternak, journalist William L. Shirer, U.S. President Richard Nixon (Venus), Sir Robert Baden-Powell, model Christine Keeler, occultist Sybil Leek, actor Peter Fonda, actress Drew Barrymore.

4 Pisces

Shylock, the merchant of Venice. A weaker degree. These people seem severe in their judgment and more critical of others. Not very Piscean. Possibly an occult or mystical influence or a desire to be celibate. A monk. Music.

Examples: friar Junipera Serra (Jupiter), singer Leonard Cohen (Moon), theologian Cotton Mather, Baron Rothchild, piano manufacturer Heinrich Steinway, entertainer Shelley Berman.

5 Pisces

A less important degree. These people can have emotional problems in relationships. They are quick learners. The fast student.

Examples: inventor Ben Franklin (Moon), artist Winslow Homer, musician George Harrison, author Adelle Davis.

6 Pisces

This is a stronger and more successful degree. They are capable of deep learning and concentration. Person of genius. They have that moody nature typical of many Pisceans. But music is possible here. Comedy.

Examples: astronomer Galileo, artist Renoir, artist Honore Daumier, philosopher-historian Benedetto Croce, scientist Jonas Salk (Moon), mystic Meher Baba, author Anthony Burgess, politician John Foster Dulles, singer Fats Domino, musician Johnny Cash (Sun and Mercury), singer Billie Holiday (Venus), actor Jacky Gleason, actor Jim Backus.

7 Pisces

Easy come, easy go. Many ups and downs, especially with finances. Usually quite practical, though.

Examples: architect Frank Lloyd Wright (Jupiter), author Victor Hugo, philosopher Rudolf Steiner, pioneer Buffalo Bill, actress Elizabeth Taylor (Sun and Mercury), politician Ariel Sharon.

8 Pisces

Born with a silver spoon in his mouth. They enjoy good fortune. Fixed star Skat. A strong area for music. Still there is something childish and unsure here. Can be a poet.

Examples: actress Ellen Terry, actress Joan Bennett, actress Joanne Woodward, actress Maria Schneider, author John Steinbeck, actor Leonardo DiCaprio (Jupiter), fashion designer Victoria Beckham (Jupiter), singer Lady Gaga (Jupiter), singer Whitney Houston (Ascendant), businesswoman Paris Hilton (Mars), composer Bizet (Uranus), singer Enrico Caruso, poet H.W. Longfellow, philosopher Ernest Renan, activist Ralph Nader.

9 Pisces

Sad Sack. People with this degree often lack confidence. Nevertheless, there is generally a sweet personality and often artistic talent. Models. There is also a touch of melancholy. Astrology.

Examples: actress Dinah Shore, actress Bernadette Peters, astrologer Robert Pelletier (Sun and Jupiter), author Edgar Allen Poe (Moon and Venus), gangster Bugsy Siegel, jurist Hugo Black.

10 Pisces

A strong astrology degree. This degree is capable of much enlightenment. Music. A superior power and intuition shines through in this degree. The best of Pisces emerges here, its compassion and helpfulness. They love to sport. They are loyal and conscientious. Devoted to loved ones. Moreover, they have a lot of energy. The enlightened one.

Examples: astronomer Copernicus, poet Pierre de Ronsard (Moon), composer Chopin, singer Enrico Caruso (Mercury), singer Harry Belafonte, singer Roger Daltry, composer Dmitri Shostakovich (Saturn), U.S. President Abraham Lincoln (Mercury), activist Martin Luther King (Venus), author John Irving.

11 Pisces

Often someone who "misses the boat." Perhaps they are too freedom-loving. At any rate, they are also marvelously self-sufficient. Astrology.

Examples: composer Bedrich Smetana, composer Kurt Weill, politician Mikhail Gorbachev, singer Karen Carpenter, actress Jennifer Jones, actress Elizabeth Jagger.

12 Pisces

The sensualist. A lovable but also sexual degree of Pisces. All of the arts are a possibility. Love of animals. A business side.

Examples: actress Jean Harlow, author Henry Miller (Jupiter), politician Silvio Berlusconi (Moon), industrialist Ivar Kreugar, inventor Alexander Graham Bell, champion bridge player Charles Goren, musician Jon Bon Jovi.

13 Pisces

These people are sometimes confusing or deceptive. An actor's degree. The thespian. Business.

Examples: playwright Oscar Wilde (Neptune), singer Enrico Caruso (Mercury), actress Paula Prentiss, fashion designer Pierre Cardin (Uranus), actor Jason Robards (Uranus), politician Aleksei Kosygin.

14 Pisces

This is a business degree and fairly lucky. But some of these people are a bit shady, while others are materialistic and not always honest. The petty thief. Yet there is something gentle and congenial in the character as well.

Examples: activist George Lincoln Rockwell (Mercury), composer Vivaldi, singer Billie Holiday (Jupiter), coach Knute Rockne, actor Rex Harrison, actor Charlie Sheen (Saturn).

15 Pisces

A rather aggressive degree for Pisces. The schoolyard bully. Nor are they particularly organized. Some desire to travel. Music.

Examples: composer Handel, composer Franz Schubert (Jupiter), author Shelley (Moon), poet Elizabeth Browning, singer Mary Wilson, author Gabriel Garcia Marquez.

16 Pisces

A chip on his shoulder. Another musical degree. There is a desire for knowledge. Devotion to home and family. Yet these people are not very trusting; they can be suspicious, defensive, and resentful.

Examples: composer Maurice Ravel, aritst Piet Mondrian, actress Anna Magnani, artist Carel Willink, actor Daniel Travanti.

17 Pisces

Sink or swim. This is a weak degree. Perhaps they are too dependent on others.

Examples: botanist Luther Burbank, cosmonaut Yuri Gagarin, author Mickey Spillane, activist George Lincoln Rockwell, author Bret Easton Ellis.

18 Pisces

A very strong degree, if not altogether violent and aggressive. This degree can make a strategist. The chess player. They have both energy and intelligence.

Examples: politician Vyacheslav Molotov, author Yukio Mishima (Uranus), chess master Bobby Fischer, Salvation Army founder William B. Booth, Oliver Wendell Holmes Jr., actress Juliette Binoche.

19 Pisces

Various all-around abilities. A philosopher, a lover of wisdom. Or a writer or a great reader. Often some genius for business. They should be careful of what they eat because they may develop digestive ailments. "Our great and glorious masterpiece is to live properly."—Montaigne.

Examples: Emperor Marcus Aurelius (Venus), author Michel de Montaigne, scientist Sir Isaac Newton (Saturn), theologian Cardinal Richelieu (Moon), activist Martin Luther King (Moon), author Joseph Conrad (Neptune), author Victoria Sackville-West, businessman Leland Stanford, band leader Lawrence Welk, actor Chuck Norris, actress Sharon Stone, terrorist Osama bin Laden.

20 Pisces

John-a-dreams. This is a soft and sympathetic degree in Pisces. They tend to float off in a world of fantasy at times. Music. On the other hand they may have an aggressive side as well.

Examples: composer Franz Schubert (Moon), singer Nina Hagen, media mogul Rupert Murdoch, politician Harold Wilson, activist Ralph Abernathy, Prince Edward, murderer James Earl Ray.

21 Pisces

Sharp-toothed unkindness. This is probably the only degree in Pisces that is associated with cruelty. They can be tricky and deceptive. They work in secrecy. Possibly a criminal. Adventurous. Yet also energetic and sociable.

Examples: war criminal Ratko Mladic, dancer Vaslav Nijinsky, poet Gabriele D'Annunzio, author Jack Kerouac, singer Liza Minnelli, musician Al Jarreau.

22 Pisces

A person with complexes. Many of these people have emotional problems and entanglements with their relationships. Yet there is also much creativity here.

Examples: composer Hugo Wolf, playwright Edward Albee, humorist Max Shulman, musician James Taylor, astronomer Percival Lowell.

23 Pisces

The crying game. Probably the most brilliant degree in Pisces. The stroke of genius. $E = mc^2$. Can be both scientific or musical.

These natives can be very inspired, but they seem to receive their share of suffering as well. Fixed star Markab.

Examples: mathematician Albert Einstein, physician Havelock Ellis (Neptune), actor Peter Sellers (Uranus), artist Ferdinand Holder, actor Michael Caine, actor-director Billy Crystal, composer Johann Strauss, musician Ry Cooder, comedian Richard Pryor (Ascendant).

24 Pisces

People with this degree often have artistic talent and are usually over-sexed. Painting is especially favored. Their weaknesses are over-indulgence and deception. A drinker.

Examples: author Sidonie-Gabrielle Colette (Venus), artist Michelangelo, Victor Eugene Delacroix (Venus), artist Gauguin (Saturn), artist Seurat (Neptune), U.S. President Andrew Jackson, murderer Josef Mengele, cartoonist Hank Ketcham, musician Quincy Jones.

25 Pisces

A violent and rebellious degree of Pisces. The revolutionary. Brave and stubborn. Artistic ability.

Examples: politician Robespierre (Uranus), philosopher Karl Marx (Pluto), author Henry David Thoreau (Pluto), author Gertrude Stein (Mars), murderer John Wayne Gacy, athlete O. J. Simpson (Moon), author Victor Hugo (Mercury), artist Rosa Bonheur, musician Nat King Cole, director Bernardo Bertolucci, entertainer Jerry Lewis (Sun and Uranus), dancer Rudolph Nureyev.

26 Pisces

The emotional fish. Very rebellious, but hard-working as well. This is an occult degree and could indicate an astrologer. The most noble traits of Pisces return in this degree and the following one. Often a desire to help humanity. All the arts are also a possibility. Usually deep, philosophical, and high-minded; but there are shallow types as well. Moreover, they can be obsessive.

Examples: First Lady Patricia Nixon, actor Patrick Duffy, actor Kurt Russell, U.S. President James Madison, astronomer Copernicus (Mercury), philosopher Nietzsche (Jupiter).

27 Pisces

Another occult degree. A desire to help others. The true humanitarian. Astrology. Often literary. Yet there is also a childish and naive side to the nature. Perhaps politics.

Examples: occultist Manly Palmer Hall, poet Stephane Mallarme, actor George Plimpton, U.S. President Grover Cleveland, politician Neville Chamberlain, explorer Amerigo Vespucci, composer Nikolai Rimsky-Korsakov, musician Andres Segovia, singer Venessa L. Williams.

28 Pisces

An intelligent mind capable of serious study. The occult. Generally financially fortunate. Often receives an excellent education. Ivy League. Yet this clever mind may also be used for more ulterior purposes. Fixed star Scheat.

Examples: missionary David Livingstone, explorer Richard Burton, jurist Earl Warren, author Philip Roth, author John Updike, author Irving Wallace, astrologer Raphael I, psychic Edgar Cayce, actress Ursula Andress, actor Bruce Willis, actress Glenn Close, military leader Alfred von Tirpitz, architect Albert Speer, murderer Adolf Eichmann, murderer Sirhan Sirhan.

29 Pisces

This is a strange degree. Sometimes spiritual, intuitive, or psychic. Often weak and dreamy. There is something fatalistic here and at times this degree has been connected with suicide. The final effort. The last day of winter. "To be or not to be—that is the question."—Hamlet.

Examples: astrologer Sepharial, psychic Elsie Wheeler (Moon), playwright Henrik Ibsen, politician William Jennings Bryan, composer Gustav Mahler (Neptune), author Jack Kerouac (Venus), psychiatrist R.D. Laing (Ascendant), murderer Marie LaLaurie.

www.ingramcontent.com/pod-product-compliance
Lightning Source LLC
Chambersburg PA
CBHW032104080426
42733CB00006B/413